Leckie × Leckie

Scotland's leading educational publishers

D0276005

#1 FOR REVISION

National 5
ENGLISH
SUCCESS GUIDE

N5 ENGLISH SUCCESS GUIDE

Iain Valentine

001/18092013

10 9 8 7 6 5 4 3 2 1

ISBN 9780007504855

Published by
Leckie & Leckie Ltd
An imprint of HarperCollins*Publishers*
Westerhill Road, Bishopbriggs, Glasgow, G64 2QT
T: 0844 576 8126   F: 0844 576 8131
leckieandleckie@harpercollins.co.uk   www.leckieandleckie.co.uk

Special thanks to
Donna Cole (copy-edit); QBS (layout); Ink Tank (cover design); Delphine Lawrance (proofread); Jill Laidlaw (proofread)

Printed in Italy by Lego, S.P.A.

A CIP Catalogue record for this book is available from the British Library.

Acknowledgements
Information on pages 8, 14, 18, 22, 57, 68, 69 and 70 © Scottish Qualifications Authority; extract from *Sherlock* on page 9 was reproduced by permission of Hartswood Films/Steven Moffat; extract from *Going to Sea in a Sieve* by Danny Baker on page 11 was reproduced with permission of Orion Books; extracts 'The Men Behind the Morphsuit' by Tom Lamont on pages 12–13 and 'Will the Paralympics stop you staring at me?' by Paul Carter on pages 28–29 were reproduced by permission of Guardian Newspapers; poem 'Introduction to Poetry' from *The Apple that Astonished Paris* by Billy Collins on pages 20–21 was reproduced with permission of Enitharmon Press; extract from 'Friday's Local Heroes: Renicks eager to take sister act to Glasgow' by Richard Winton was reproduced by permission of Herald & Times Group; extract from *Bold Girls* by Rona Munro on pages 40–43 was reproduced by permission of Hodder Education; extract from 'The Telegram', by Iain Crichton Smith on pages 44–46 was reproduced by permission of Birlinn Ltd; extract from 'All that Glisters', by Anne Donovan on pages 48–49 was reproduced by permission of Canongate Books; poem 'Originally' by Carol Ann Duffy on pages 50–51 was reproduced by permission of Picador; poem 'Sounds of the Day', by Norman MacCaig on page 55 was reproduced by permission of Birlinn Ltd.

We would like to thank the following for permission to reproduce photographs. Page numbers are followed, where necessary, by t (top), b (bottom), m (middle), l (left) or r (right).

P7 lightpoet; p8 iStockphoto; p9 iStockphoto; p11 iStockphoto; p12 Guardian Newspapers/Ross Gilmore; p15 Jetta Productions; p18tl Monkey Business Images; p18tr Hemera; p18bl iStockphoto; p18br iStockphoto; p20l Wavebreak Media; p20m iStockphoto; p20r iStockphoto; p24 Lifesize; p28 mezzotint; p34 Herald & Times Group/Steve Cox; p38 Canongate Books; p52 Strat Mastoris/NVT; p44 Milos Luzanin; p48 Pixel Memoirs; p50 Pojoslaw; p54 Design Pics; p63 Igor Bulgarin; p64 iStockphoto; p66 iStockphoto; p68 Tatiana Popova; p72 Image source; p74 Wavebreak Media; 76t Photodisc; p76m iStockphoto; p76b Digital Vision; p77 iStockphoto; p78 Digital Vision

Contents

Chapter 4: The question paper: Critical reading – Scottish texts

Chapter 5: The question paper: critical reading – the critical essay

Chapter 6: The writing portfolio

Introduction

National 5 English

National 5 English is a new qualification for candidates in Scottish schools, which gives you the opportunity to build on what you have already learned in school with the Curriculum for Excellence. It replaces Intermediate 2 English and Standard Grade English at Credit level. It is a skills-based course that aims to develop your listening, talking, reading and writing skills (*literacy* skills and *thinking* skills). These skills are fundamental to your future. Success at National 5 will increase the choices open to you in life. Doing well at this level will allow you to get that job or training place you want; get access to college courses or progress to Higher English. This book will tell you all you need to know about how to prepare for your exam and how to maximise your chances of success.

Course structure

The National 5 English course consists of **two** units that all candidates must complete. These are:

- **Analysis and evaluation**
- **Creation and production**

In order to achieve the course award, you must pass *both* of these units *and* the external assessment (the question paper and the portfolio of writing).

Analysis and evaluation unit

The **analysis and evaluation unit** has two outcomes.

> **Outcome 1**
> You have to understand, analyse and evaluate at least one detailed written text (a *reading* task).
>
>
>
> **Outcome 2**
> You have to understand, analyse and evaluate at least one detailed spoken language activity (a *listening* task).
>
>

Creation and production unit

The **creation and production unit** also has two outcomes.

> **Outcome 1**
> You will have to create at least one written text using detailed written language.
>
>

Outcome 2

You will have to create at least one spoken interaction using detailed language (giving an individual talk or taking part in a group discussion). You will see what is meant by 'detailed' language later in the book.

Assessment

These unit outcomes will all be assessed by the English teachers at your school. You can be reassessed in anything you don't pass first time.

The **external assessment** for the course consists of a question paper (the exam) and a writing portfolio.

The question paper is made up of two sections.

- The first section is called **reading for understanding, analysis and evaluation** and it is worth 30 marks. You will be asked to read **a passage of non-fiction** and then answer a series of **questions on the passage**. You should be familiar with this kind of 'close reading' from your work in English during S1–S3 and/or in your National 4 course.

- The second section of the question paper is called **critical reading** and has two parts. It is worth 40 marks. In the first part you will answer questions on a **Scottish text** you have studied as part of the National 5 course (20 marks). In the second part you will have to write one **critical essay** about a play, novel, short story, poem, film or TV programme you have studied in class as part of the National 5  course (20 marks). You cannot use the same text in both parts and your answer in part 2 must cover a different genre from the text you answered on in part 1.

The **writing portfolio** is worth 30 marks (30% of your total mark) so it is really important that you devote your time and energy to sending away the *best* material that you can. Remember, this is the one part of the assessment that is entirely under your control. You will submit two pieces of writing to be marked by the SQA. One of the pieces has to be **creative** (a story, a poem, a piece of drama, etc.). The other piece has to be **discursive** (persuasive or argumentative). You will already have experience of these types of writing from your work in S1–S3 and/or at National 4.

Reading skills

In order to pass this unit you will need to be able to identify what the writer is **trying to do in a text** and **who the text is aimed at**. You also have to show that you can **identify** the main points being made (often by summarising them) and that you can also **infer** things from the text. The text you are asked to 'understand, analyse and evaluate' in the assessment of this unit might be a piece of fiction (novel or short story), a piece of non-fiction, an advert, a blog …

in fact it could be anything that could be described as a 'detailed written text'.

Here is the assessment grid that your teacher/tutor will use to assess your performance. Your answers (which can be written or spoken) need to show you can do all of the things indicated in the grid.

National 5: Understand, analyse and evaluate *detailed* written texts.	Identify and explain the purpose and audience as appropriate to genre.
	Identify and explain the main ideas and supporting details.
	Apply knowledge and understanding of language to explain meaning and effect, using appropriate critical terminology.

SQA 2012

In the pages that follow, we will look at the skills you need to develop. National 5 puts particular emphasis on your ability to *infer* and to *summarise* – two key skills that you need to develop in this course.

Reading skills: how to infer things

Being able to *infer* something means working it out without actually being told it. It's all about looking for clues and then using them to arrive at the answer.

For example, if you walk into someone's house for the first time and in the hallway you see a bowl filled with dog food and a dog's lead hanging up, then it would be reasonable to *infer* that the person you are visiting owns a dog.

Here is an extract from the script of the TV drama series, *Sherlock*. Look how Sherlock Holmes is able to infer things about Dr Watson from their first meeting.

Sherlock Holmes:	I'm a consulting detective. Only one in the world. I invented the job.
Watson:	What does that mean?
Sherlock Holmes:	It means when the police are out of their depth, which is always, they consult me.
Watson:	The police don't consult amateurs.
Sherlock Holmes:	When I met you for the first time yesterday, I said Afghanistan or Iraq. You looked surprised.
Watson:	Yes, how did you know?
Sherlock Holmes:	I didn't know, I saw. Your haircut, the way you hold yourself says military. And your conversation as you entered the room …
Watson:	A bit different from my day.
Sherlock Holmes:	… said trained at Barts – so army doctor. Obvious. Your face is tanned but no tan above the wrists. You've been abroad, but not sunbathing. Your limp's really bad when you walk, but you don't ask for a chair when you stand. Like you've forgotten about it, so it's at least partly psychosomatic. That says the original circumstances of the injury were traumatic. Wounded in action, suntan – Afghanistan or Iraq?
Watson:	You said I had a therapist.
Sherlock Holmes:	You've got a psychosomatic limp, of course you've got a therapist. Then there's your brother. Your phone. It's expensive, email enabled, MP3 player. You're looking for a flatshare. You wouldn't waste money on this – it's a gift then. Scratches. Not just one, many over time. It's been in the same pocket as keys and coins. The man sitting next to me wouldn't treat his one luxury item like this. So it's had a previous owner. Next bit's easy. You know it already.
	'Harry Watson – from Clara x x x'

Chapter 1: The analysis and evaluation unit

Watson: The engraving?

Sherlock Holmes: Harry Watson – clearly a family member who's given you his old phone. Not your father – this is a young man's gadget. Could be a cousin, but you're a war hero who can't find a place to live. Unlikely you've got an extended family, certainly not one you're close to, so brother it is. Now, Clara – who's Clara? Three kisses says it's romantic attachment. The expense of the phone says wife, not girlfriend. Must've given it to him recently – this model's only six months old. Marriage in trouble then – six months on he's just given it away. If she'd left *him*, he would have kept it. People do, sentiment. But *no*, he wanted rid of it – he left *her*. He gave the phone to you, that says he wants you to stay in touch. You're looking for cheap accommodation and you're not going to your brother for help? That says you've got problems with him. Maybe you liked his wife, maybe you don't like his drinking.

Watson: How can you possibly know about the drinking?

Sherlock Holmes: Shot in the dark. Good one, though. Power connection – tiny little scuff marks round the edge. Every night he goes to plug it in and charge but his hands are shaking. You never see those marks on a sober man's phone, never see a drunk's without them.

(From *Sherlock*, 'A Study in Pink', Hartswood Films/Steven Moffat)

Being able to *infer* things when you are reading involves you making use of the clues in the text: just like Sherlock Holmes does.

Read the following passage carefully and, just like Sherlock Holmes, see if you can **infer** the answers to the following questions. Make a note of the **clues** you use to make your deductions. Check your answers on page 80.

> I am seven years old and the car in which I sit is, by now, totally enveloped in flames. The old banger had had a good run. Ever since we had found it abandoned on our dump – in the 1960s, bombsites were called 'dumps' – we had been using it as a kind of base camp.
> 5   Now, with its slashed front seats exposing clumps of horse-hair, together with the plywood tea chests we had squeezed into the rear after the seats were removed, it seemed to almost beg for a playful match. So we had all piled in, popped a Swan Vesta and declared whoever got out first was a coward and whoever stayed till last was
> 10   the game's winner. I know, I know. And kids these days make all that fuss about Nintendo.

On fire for about ten minutes now, it was clearly no longer a matter of when I should get out but whether I could get out. But I wasn't moving. Not yet. Not me. The tea chest in which I squatted was

15 starting to give off thin wisps of smoke that foretold, any second now, it would probably go up in a huge fireball. Still I was determined to win. Besides, other than me, there was only Pete left inside this blazing wreck and Kingy was certainly no champion when it came to a rattling good game of chicken like this. He would definitely lose

20 his nerve before long – I mean, I had to believe that or what was the point of the whole exercise?

We looked at each other defiantly, head and shoulders poking up above the tin-lined edges of our tea chests, the flames now billowing along the roof of the rusted old vehicle, the smoke funnelling out

25 through where once had been doors on the doomed Ford Popular. The thick plume billowed across the bombsite.

The front of the car had predictably gone up like a gasworks, disqualifying Tommy Hodges, Stephen Micalef and Tony Plumpton almost immediately as they panicked and leapt out, it seemed to me,

30 prematurely. They hadn't lasted ten seconds. Now it was down to just Kingy and me. And though I daren't show it, yes I was beginning to find the growing inferno's repeated metallic bangs, pops and fizzes a tad alarming. But did he?

Of course what neither I nor

35 Kingy, nor any of our half-dozen or so friends cheering us on from the relative safety of three feet away, had entertained for a moment

40 was the idea that there might still be a petrol tank lurking within the old banger.

And it was growing fearsomely hot in there…

Danny Baker, *Going to Sea in a Sieve*

	Clues	Answer
1. Where is this passage set?		
2. Who do you think 'we' are?		
3. What is a Swan Vesta?		
4. Why is Pete referred to as Kingy?		
5. What is a Ford Popular?		
6. From what sort of text is this passage taken?		

Reading skills: how to summarise texts

Being able to **summarise** text simply means being able to identify the main points made by the writer and then to sum them up in your own words. You might be asked to summarise information found within a single paragraph, or from within a longer section of text. If you are asked to consider more than one paragraph in a non-fiction passage, it is a good idea to look first at the **topic sentence** of each paragraph – the sentence that gives the clearest idea of what the paragraph is about. This is often (but not always) the first sentence in each paragraph. Your summary should include only the most important details.

Read the following passage and summarise it in no more than **seven** bullet points.

Check your answers on page 81.

The men behind the morphsuit

It started out as a hilarious prank at a stag-do and has morphed into a million-pound fancy dress phenomenon. Tom Lamont meets the three Scotsmen who have given the world the mighty morphsuit.

Shape of things to come: revellers cover up in a selection of morphsuits at the T in the Park festival in Kinross.

Not long ago, three friends from Scotland went out for drinks wearing brightly coloured costumes from Japan. It would prove a pivotal night of fancy dress.

The trio – brothers Ali and Fraser Smeaton, and their friend from
5   Edinburgh University, Gregor Lawson – were skiing in Canada. They decided to hit the local bars wearing 'zentai suits' – skin-tight Japanese leotards that covered them from head to toe. It was an

10   idea Gregor had pinched from a stag weekend, where one of the attendees, newly back from Asia, had shown up in a vivid blue zentai. 'Everyone wanted to buy him a drink,' recalls Gregor. 'I'd never seen anything like it.'

15   In Canada, dressed up in zentai suits of their own, the trio were likewise admired. 'The resort shut down, people were stopping us in the street,' says Ali Smeaton. The friends wondered if they'd stumbled on a way to make some cash – perhaps fund next year's ski trip. 'A bit of pocket money,' says Ali. 'We'd take something that existed, give it a name, change certain physical elements, bring it to the masses.' One modification they decided on right away was that their version would be made of something more see-through.

20   They'd been walking around virtually blind.

25   That was in early 2009. Today, the morphsuit (as the trio boozily agreed to name their product) is a multimillion-pound concern. A zip-up costume made of polyester and Lycra, all-enveloping so that the wearer looks like a featureless mannequin, the morphsuit has become commonplace at sporting events and stag nights, festivals and parties. It has also made unusual incursions into the world beyond. The day after Bin Laden was killed, in 2011, Al Jazeera carried a photograph of an anonymous American celebrating outside the White House in a morphsuit patterned with stars and

30   stripes.

35   The Smeatons and Gregor hear of barely credible use of their creation almost every day. In the first week of July there were morphsuits spotted at the European Championships in Kiev (where three Italian football fans in the red, white and green of *il tricolore* watched their team lose) and at the Olympic torch relay in Warwick (a lone man in an all-body union flag watching the flame pass). Police in Gloucestershire warned of a man acting suspiciously in a morphsuit in the Forest of Dean. At the same

40   time, Ali, Fraser and Gregor – now in their early 30s, together known as AFG Media – made national news when they secured £4.2m in funding to expand their business. It already had a projected annual turnover of £11m.

The Observer, August 2012

EXAM TIP

This is an easy skill to practise. You can take virtually any newspaper article and identify the main points within it. Try to do this regularly (once or twice a week) with articles from quality newspapers.

Reading skills: identifying and analysing

In order to pass this unit you will need to use your knowledge of language features.

National 5: Understand, analyse and evaluate *detailed* written texts.	Identify and explain the purpose and audience as appropriate to genre.
	Identify and explain the main ideas and supporting details.
	Apply knowledge and understanding of language to explain meaning and effect, using appropriate critical terminology.

SQA 2012

Such features include *word choice, sentence structure, imagery, tone, sound* – all things you should have come across in your Broad General Education in S1–S3. You should be able to identify the following language features relating to imagery and sound.

Imagery (used by writers to create pictures in the reader's mind using words)

- **Simile** – a comparison using the words 'like' or 'as … as'.
- **Metaphor** – a comparison in which something is called something else – think of it as a 'stronger' comparison than a simile.
- **Personification** – a special type of metaphor in which something that is not human is given human qualities.

Sound

- **Alliteration** – consonant sounds repeated at the start of a number of words.
- **Onomatopoeia** – words that sound like their meaning.

You should be able to spot all of these five techniques in the following text. Check your answers on page 81.

It was another grey day in the great prison where David was four years into a six-year sentence. As he listened to the buzz of classroom voices around him, he felt his mind slipping away like a ship being launched into the sea. But the dark figure of mathematics wouldn't let him escape, and soon chased after him.

Sentence structure

You must also be aware of techniques and language features relating to sentence structure.

You should be able to identify the following language features:

- **List** – look for sequences of single words or longer expressions.
- **Minor sentence** – an incomplete sentence (a sentence without a finite verb).
- **Short sentence** – often used for impact or emphasis.
- **Repetition** – look for repeated words, expressions or structures.
- **Climax** – words or expressions building to a high point.
- **Anti-climax** – the writer seems to be building to a high point but adds something to deliberately weaken the effect, often to create a comic effect.
- **Rhetorical question** – question asked to create an effect rather than to seek information.
- **Parenthesis** – extra information inserted into a sentence.
- **Inversion** – where the usual word order of a sentence is turned around to highlight particular words or expressions.
- **Juxtaposition** – where words are placed together to achieve a particular effect (when two words of *opposite* meaning are placed together you get an oxymoron, e.g. bitter sweet; old news).
- **Punctuation** (including comma, colon, semi-colon, inverted commas, etc.) – see the table on pages 16–17.

Punctuation	Use	Examples
Comma ,	To separate items in a list.	Lewis, Neil, Colin and I all went to the match.
	To mark parenthesis.	The dancers, all under twenty-five, ignored the onlooker.
	To separate clauses in a sentence.	That night we went to the club, which turned out to be a good decision.
Colon :	To introduce a quotation.	The school motto remained burned in her memory: 'This is the way to the stars!'
	To introduce a list.	Memories flooded back: the meal; the film; the walk home and the painful goodbye.
	To introduce an explanation or expansion.	The Scots were unlucky: two shots hit the bar.
Semi-colon ;	To separate statements that are closely connected or to act as a 'hinge' in a balanced sentence.	Hibs played well; Hearts were poor.
	To separate longer expressions in a list.	All the ingredients for a successful study session were in place: a quiet room; revision materials to hand; healthy snacks; appropriate music.
Single dash –	To highlight what follows by separating it from the rest of the sentence.	Up ahead of them was their greatest challenge – the steepest rock of the climb.
	To add an afterthought.	She was the most popular girl in the class – at least that's what she believed.
Paired dash – – or **Brackets** ( )	To indicate extra information within a sentence (parenthesis).	The exam – National 5 History – was harder than expected.
Inverted commas ' ... '	To mark direct speech.	'Are you sure?' she asked.
	To indicate titles.	'Kidnapped' is one of the Scottish texts for National 5 English.
	To suggest words are being used in a particular way, e.g. to suggest irony.	The police 'assisted' the troublesome fan away from the ground.
Question mark ?	To indicate a question.	Why do we make pupils sit exams?
Exclamation mark !	To mark an exclamation.	The class continued to behave badly – and that was after the head teacher had been in to see them!
	To indicate surprise, shock or someone shouting in direct speech.	'Come on Scotland!' she yelled.

Ellipsis ...	To indicate missing words in a sentence.	We could go to the …'
	To indicate where a speaker breaks off without completing a sentence.	The sheer number of apps available on your phone: Twitter, Facebook …
	To suggest a list could be continued.	Instagram, Angry Birds … means that there are more and more ways to avoid real work.

Other language features you might be expected to recognise and comment on include:

- **Hyperbole or exaggeration** – to overstate something for effect – are common feature of persuasive writing.
- **Contrast** – to emphasise difference by comparing opposite or dissimilar things. Always make sure you refer to *both* sides of the contrast.

Quick Test

Check your answers on page 82.

1. Identify the language features used in the following sentences.
   (a) She went as white as a sheet with fright.
   (b) He was tired: tired of the late nights; tired of the arguments; tired of everything.
   (c) The blood oozed from under the door.
   (d) As he approached the building – it looked dirtier now he was close up – he began to think about the meeting.
   (e) She switched on the engine. The metal monster snarled into life.
   (f) Softly, slowly, they approached the door.
   (g) The Sun smiled on the crowded beach.
   (h) His head was aching. It felt like someone was hammering nails into his temple.
   (i) It was getting closer and closer. It was getting louder and louder. He looked up. High above his head was the alien spaceship.
   (j) Why should we be made to revise for exams? Wouldn't it be better if all exams were abolished?
   (k) What a goal!
   (l) The water gurgled down the drain.
   (m) Never again.
   (n) The purple parrots played in the park.
   (o) She remembered what she had to buy: a pint of milk; a *Daily Record*; six eggs; butter; that jam her mum liked.

2. Have a look at the following texts and see how many language features you can spot. You should also comment on the *effect* created by the writer.
   (a) He looked ahead and watched the flames burning brightly. There was no way he could cross the bridge. No way. Not today. Not tomorrow. Not ever.
   (b) He watched in the school canteen as she got closer and closer. He could almost hear his heart thumping louder and louder. His opportunity was here at last. 'Would you… would you… would you pass me the salt, please?' he stammered.
   (c) Is it right that we are to be made to wear uniforms? What about our individuality? What about our freedom to choose?
   (d) Excitedly I made my way back to the car (a gleaming silver BMW) and got in. I loved everything about it: the leather upholstery; the tinted windows; the powerful engine and the satisfying roar it made as I travelled through the streets of the city.

17

Listening skills

Think about all the different kinds of listening you do each day.

Listening is not part of your external exam but you do have to show that you can *understand, analyse and evaluate **detailed** spoken language* in order to pass one of the outcomes in the analysis and evaluation unit.

Let's look at exactly what you have to do to pass this outcome.

When you are being assessed in listening, there are a number of things you have to do to achieve the outcome at National 5. The SQA has put these in the following table.

National 5: Understand, analyse and evaluate ***detailed*** spoken language.	2.1 Identify and explain the purpose and audience as appropriate to genre.
	2.2 Identify and explain the main ideas and supporting details.
	2.3 Apply knowledge and understanding of language to explain meaning and effect, using appropriate critical terminology.

SQA 2012

Whichever kind of detailed spoken language you have been asked to listen to, you must work out what the speaker is trying to do. For example, is the speaker (remember it might be someone talking to you in person or you might be watching or listening to a video or audio text) trying to:

- Give you information about something?
- Warn you about something?
- Entertain you?
- Persuade you about something?

The more listening practice you do, the more confident you will become in being able to *deduce* the speaker's purpose.

To deduce the audience the spoken language is aimed at, think about who would be interested in hearing it. Consider their:

- **Age** – is the language more appropriate for older or younger people?
- **Background** – is the communication aimed at people with a particular social position or education?
- **Interests** – does the communication contain specialised content or is it aimed at the general public?
- **Gender** – is the communication aimed at a male audience or a female audience or both men and women?

In addition to these aspects of spoken language, you need to be aware of the differences between the language of, for example, a news report and a piece of advertising. Don't forget that you also need to understand what is being said and also work out things from any clues in the spoken language.

Finally, you have to be able to comment on any language techniques used by the speaker in much the same way that you do when analysing a piece of writing. Remember you are using exactly the same skills for this as you do when you analyse a 'detailed written text' for the other outcome in this unit.

This sounds like a lot to do, but remember that the questions given to you by your teacher/lecturer when you are being assessed on listening will guide you through each of these elements. You will be allowed to give your answers in spoken form or in writing.

The BBC website is a useful source of practice material; in particular the BBC Learning Zone at http://www.bbc.co.uk/learningzone/clips/. You can practise your listening skills by selecting a video clip, watching and listening to it carefully and then asking yourself the following questions.

1. (a) Who would be interested in watching this video clip?
   (b) Give a reason for your answer.
2. (a) What is the purpose of the video clip?
   (b) Give a reason for your answer.
3. Identify **three** main points made in the video.
4. Identify **two** parts of the video where you think language is being used in a special way. For example, does the tone of the speaker's voice change at all? Are there any questions or exclamations used in the spoken language? Are there individual words or phrases that are used to achieve particular effects?
5. (a) Did the video keep you interested in its subject?
   (b) Give a reason for your answer.

Practice unit assessment: analysis and evaluation – reading

There are many ways in which you may be asked to show that you have met the criteria to pass this unit outcome. You might be given an assessment as part of a longer unit of work or a 'stand alone' test like the one here.

No matter what form the assessment takes, the questions will give you the opportunity to demonstrate the skills you need to pass. You might be asked to write down your answers or to say them out loud to your teacher. You might be asked to type your answers. Whichever method is chosen, your teacher will keep a record of the answers that you give as assessment evidence.

Read the following poem carefully and then answer the questions that follow.

Introduction to Poetry

I ask them to take a poem
and hold it up to the light
like a color slide

or press an ear against its hive.

5   I say drop a mouse into a poem
and watch him probe his way out,

or walk inside the poem's room
and feel the walls for a light switch.

I want them to waterski
10   across the surface of a poem
waving at the author's name on the shore.

But all they want to do
is tie the poem to a chair with rope
and torture a confession out of it.

15   They begin beating it with a hose
to find out what it really means.
Billy Collins

The questions are designed to show that you have met the assessment criteria.
Compare your answers with those in the table on page 83.

1. Who would be likely to read this poem?

   (a) Think about:
   - age and/or
   - interests and/or
   - background.

   (b) Explain how you reached this conclusion.

2. Who do you think the speaker in the poem is?

3. Who do you think 'them' and 'they' are?

4. **(a)** Explain – in your own words – what the speaker in the poem wants 'them' to do.

   (b) Does he succeed? Find a piece of evidence to show this.

5. Choose **three** examples of the poet using a language technique to achieve a particular effect.

   (a) Identify each technique being used.

   (b) Explain what effect you think the writer is trying to achieve in each case.

6. Why do you think Billy Collins wrote this poem?

Writing skills

There's really nothing for you to be worried about with this part of the course. After all, you have been writing in one form or another since you started school. Any writing tasks you are asked to undertake for this unit will build on skills you already have. Your English courses in S1–S3 should have prepared you for writing at this level.

In order to achieve this unit outcome you will have to produce **one** piece of writing that meets criteria set by SQA.

National 5: Create and Produce **detailed** written texts.	Select significant ideas and content using a format and structure appropriate to purpose and audience.
	Apply knowledge and understanding of language in terms of language choice and technical accuracy.
	Communicate meaning at first reading.

SQA 2012

The piece of writing might be part of a larger unit of work or be an assignment on its own. You might be asked to produce:

- a short story
- an extract from a novel
- a drama script
- a persuasive essay
- an argumentative essay
- a personal reflective essay
- an information leaflet
- a blog entry.

Your teacher will tell you how and when you will be assessed.

This piece of writing has to be *detailed* and *structured effectively*. This means you will have to include enough content and also make good use of paragraphing to organise the piece.

Your *syntax* – that's just the technical term for sentence structure – has to be accurate, as does your *vocabulary*. Make sure you are using appropriate word choice for your chosen topic.

You must use a *variety of expressions*, which means that you can't just use the same type of simple sentences over and over again, and that you should use a range of language techniques appropriate to the form and genre in which you are writing. You'll be reminded of these techniques as part of your work for the reading outcome in the analysis and evaluation unit. You should always try to incorporate these techniques in your own writing.

Your writing must be fluent – smooth and flowing from sentence to sentence and paragraph to paragraph – and must convey your meaning clearly. Whoever reads it should not have to look over sections again and again in order to understand the content.

Don't forget the basics. Whatever form your writing takes, make sure you are able to punctuate it correctly. By this point in your studies you should be confident in using the following correctly and effectively:

- capital letters (it's amazing how many S4 and S5 pupils have trouble with these!)
- full stops
- commas (don't use them to join sentences together)
- inverted commas (make sure you know the conventions of indicating direct speech)
- colons
- semi-colons
- question marks
- exclamation marks
- single dashes
- paired dashes (or brackets) to indicate parenthesis.

There are further details about punctuation on pages 16–17.

The piece of writing you produce to achieve this unit outcome can be included in your writing portfolio. You will find more information on how to produce suitable pieces of writing for the portfolio in Chapter 6.

Talking skills

You don't have to do any talking in the external exam but you do need to show that you are able to take part in *detailed spoken interactions* in order to pass one of the outcomes in the creation and production unit. In other words, if you want to pass the course you must show that you can deliver an effective presentation or individual talk to an audience (and then deal with questions) *or* be an effective contributor to a group discussion.

You will already have experience of individual talk and group discussion as part of your English courses in S1–S3 and in other curricular areas. You can use the skills you have already learned to help you to pass this outcome. Lots of people, however, can still find it difficult or even a bit frightening to speak to an audience when they know they are being assessed. The trick is to always appear to be a confident individual – even when you don't always feel like that inside!

Let's look at exactly what you have to do to pass this outcome. When you give an individual talk or take part in a group discussion there are a number of things you have to do to achieve the outcome at National 5. The SQA has put these in the following table.

National 5: Take part in *detailed* spoken interactions.	Select significant ideas and content using a format and structure appropriate to purpose and audience.
	Apply knowledge and understanding of language in terms of language choice.
	Communicate meaning at first hearing.
	Use significant aspects of non-verbal communication.

SQA 2012

If you are giving an individual talk you have to make sure you have **prepared enough content** and that it contains a range of **relevant ideas** and **views**. You must also **structure your talk effectively**. Remember that you are delivering a talk, not just reading out something you have prepared and **don't wander off the topic**. The **words you choose** must **suit the purpose** of your talk (e.g. to give information; to present an argument; to talk about a personal experience). You must **speak loudly** enough so that everyone in the audience can hear what you say and try to **vary your tone of voice**.

You must not have too many hesitations and at least *appear* to be **confident** in front of the audience. Finally, remember to **look at your audience** and use **suitable body language** if that helps to get across what you are trying to say.

I	👁	**Eye**-contact
C	🔔	**C**lear
A	📣	**A**udible
N	STOP	**N**o fidgeting

Keeping eye-contact with your audience is really important. Yes, even teachers can find it difficult to look at a class of pupils (and they get paid for it!) but as long as you make the effort to do so you will have taken a significant step towards delivering a successful talk. You can look at a point in the room just above the audience if that helps.

EXAM TIP

If that seems a lot to remember, try using this simple mnemonic (left) to remind yourself what to do when you deliver the talk. (There's a bonus motivational message included for those of you who like that sort of thing!)

When Bill Clinton was President of the Unites States of America, people used to say that when he spoke to a large audience, everyone felt as if he was speaking to them as an individual.

This is a trick only the most accomplished speakers can pull off but you can do something similar by mentally dividing the room into four and then looking at each quarter in turn as you talk.

Good afternoon everyone. Today. I'm going to tell you about …If you can do this then the audience is more likely to engage with what you say.

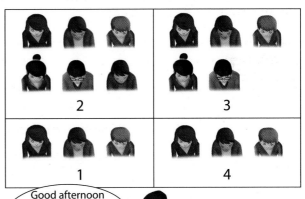

Good afternoon everyone. Today I'm going to tell you about …

Using notes

If you have prepared your talk thoroughly, then your notes should just be used to remind you about what to say next if you forget. They should be no more than bullet points of key ideas on a series of cue cards. If you were asked to talk to your audience about a work experience placement your cue cards don't need to be any more complicated than the ones on the right.

If you have prepared your talk you should be able to talk for 3 or 4 minutes quite easily.

1. MY TALK – my work experience Placement
   - Introduction
   - Where I went

2. First impressions
   - What I did each day
   - Problems I overcame

3. Amusing incidents
   - Looking back – what I learned
   - CONCLUSION
   - Does anyone have any questions?

Using slides

You can support your individual talk by using slides (for example using a slideshow program such as PowerPoint) or by using props or other audio visual aids. If you do use slides, don't forget the following:

- Don't have too much text on your slides.
- Don't just read out what's on the slides to the audience.
- Don't keep turning round to look at the screen.

My Work Experience Placement

· Three-day placement at Leckie & Leckie publishers

· Founded in 1989 – Scotland's leading educational publisher

· Specialises in textbooks, revision guides & practice exam papers for Scottish school students

Dealing with questions

Once you have finished your talk, you must ask for questions so that you can show you are *taking part in spoken interactions*. Try to answer as fully as possible. Don't just give one-word answers!

Group discussion

Taking part in *detailed spoken interactions* can also apply to a group discussion. Your teacher will probably offer you the choice of which kind of talking activity you would prefer to be assessed in.

Your teacher will use the same criteria to assess you. When you take part in group discussion you have to do the following:

- Contribute to the discussion (*range of relevant ideas/views/opinions*) – so you can't sit there in silence.

- Listen to what others say and respond to them (*take account of audience members*).

- Stick to the topic or task (*consistent, alert attention to purpose*).

- Choose words (*detailed vocabulary*) that suit the purpose of the discussion.

- Speak loudly enough so that everyone else in the group can hear what you say and try to vary your tone of voice (*audibly with expression*).

- Avoid too many hesitations and at least *appear* to be confident in front of the other members of the group (*display some fluency and confidence*).

- Remember to look at the other people round the table and use suitable body language if it helps to get across what you are trying to say (*use gesture/facial expression and eye-contact effectively*).

EXAM TIP

Here's a reminder of the skills you need to take part in a successful group discussion.
- Make sure you contribute.
- Allow others to speak.
- Listen to what others have to say.
- Speak audibly and clearly.
- Make effective use of eye-contact and gesture.
- Ask questions/challenge other speakers/ clarify or summarise what others say.

It is important that you remember about 'turn taking'. Don't talk over the other members of the group – make sure you take it in turns to speak. That doesn't mean that the discussion just goes round in a kind of circle. That can lead to a very dull discussion (top right). It is sometimes useful to go 'round the table' to clarify what people's views are but usually the best group discussion is much more complex as people summarise what others say; challenge their ideas; agree and disagree; support points that are made. That sort of discussion would look like this (bottom right).

The important thing is to let others have their say and say things yourself!

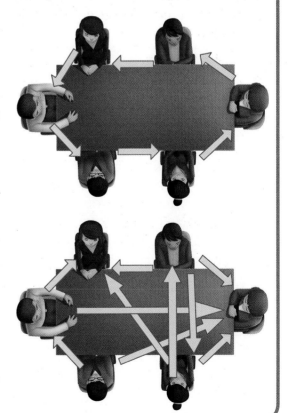

Understanding, analysis and evaluation questions

Now let's look at an example of the sort of passage and questions that you will have to deal with in the SQA examination. We'll start by looking at the first element of the question paper. This consists of a passage (non-fiction) and questions.

Remember that the questions are designed to test your understanding, analysis and evaluation of the passage.

- **Understanding** questions ask you to show your knowledge of **what** the writer is telling the reader.

- **Analysis** questions ask you to look at **how** the writer gets his or her message across.

- **Evaluation** questions ask you to decide how effective the writer's use of language is.

You can expect to be asked to **summarise** parts of the passage and to make **inferences** from its content. We'll look at both of these types of questions below.

Now read the passage that follows. It was written by Paul Carter just before the start of the Paralympic Games in London 2012. Each of the questions is followed by advice about how to answer.

> ### EXAM TIP
> Always read the **whole passage** before you start answering the questions.

Specimen passage

Will the Paralympics stop you staring at me?

1   I've been waiting seven long years for the Paralympics. I'm a wheelchair sports fan (it's the same as being an armchair sports fan except I'm more

5   portable). I've spent my entire career as a journalist and TV producer gearing up to cover a home Paralympics, and the moment is finally here.

I should probably declare a vested interest. I very nearly made it to a Paralympic Games as a competitor. But I didn't. I'm a Nearlympian, if you like. But for a small technical error with my finish, I'd have

10   gone to the Atlanta Paralympics in 1996 as a swimmer.

Before my addiction to supermarket ready-meals and cheap lager, I used to be a bit of an athlete. Sadly, at the end of my race in the national junior championships, I touched the wall with one arm rather than two. That may seem trivial, especially as I don't have

15   hands, but in the world of swimming, finishing incorrectly is treated

with as much contempt as kicking sacks of kittens into a canal. Therefore I do have a natural bitterness towards competitive sport.

20 The Paralympics have come at a very interesting time though, and have revealed a real dichotomy in public and media attitudes towards disabled people and disability in general. We may be currently surfing a wave of Games-inspired media goodwill. For the last year or two, however, coverage of us disabled types has been increasingly hostile and negative; fuelled, or at least gently encouraged, by a government keen to push its thorny agenda of welfare reform.
25 Reported hate crime against disabled people is increasing.

The word 'scroungers' has become a tabloid staple, attached to tales of disabled people living in 18-bedroom mansions and water-skiing. While there are obviously people who fiddle the system, the number is infinitesimally small compared with the column inches
30 it generates, and many disabled people, myself included, have felt tarred by the same very uncomfortable brush. Benefit has become a dirty word again, and these stories have highlighted a darker, ugly side to some sections of society that hasn't been seen in 30 years.

What's going to be interesting is watching how press coverage adapts
35 to the guaranteed success that our Paralympians will bring over the next fortnight or so. One suspects that they will be covered without any sense of irony. After all, they're different aren't they? They're superhuman. They're athletes. They're not like me, the no arms, no legs bloke who goes down the pub for five pints on a Friday.

40 Don't get me wrong. I'm not bashing the Paralympics, quite the opposite. I love them and everything they stand for. I think we're on the cusp of achieving a real change in the British public's attitude towards disabled people for the better. However, I'm not superhuman. I'm normal. In the non-pejorative sense of the word.

45 How the Paralympics affects ordinary disabled people like me is going to be fascinating. What I hope is that disability will be normalised – that people will stop staring in the street and that we'll all be accepted much more for who we are. The worst thing that could happen is that we're all suddenly treated as being amazing
50 and wonderful and brave (I obviously am, but not everyone is).

I want our Paralympians to be lauded for their talent and achievements just as much as our Olympians were – but because of those things, not in spite of their disability. Maybe, just maybe, the Paralympics will lead to a world where I can walk (OK, shuffle) down the street
55 without people thinking I'm the next David bloody Weir when I'm sneaking out for a cheeky pint and a kebab. Here's hoping.

Adapted from an article by Paul Carter in *The Guardian*, Tuesday 28 August 2012

Specimen questions and commentary

1. Look again at lines 1–6. How does the writer feel about the start of the Paralympics? Show how the writer's word choice and use of structure in these lines suggest this feeling.

   3

   The **understanding** element in this question seems very straightforward (a nice, easy question to get you started). It seems clear that the writer is *looking forward to* or *is excited* by the Paralympics. You would get 1 mark for either answer.

   Any question that asks you about **word choice** means that you must select and quote the actual words used by the writer. You could quote *'waiting seven long years'*, which suggests that idea of time passing slowly when you are looking forward to something. Or you could write down *'spent my entire career … gearing up'*, which suggests how much preparation the writer has done. Again, either example (plus a comment) would gain 1 mark. You also have to say something about **structure**: the position of the expression *'finally here'* at the end of the paragraph helps to suggest that the build-up to the event is over at last. You would gain the final mark for pointing this out.

2. What can you **infer** about the writer's swimming ability **and** his opinion of those who make the rules for competitive swimming from what you are told in the third paragraph (lines 11–17)? Support your answer with appropriate evidence.

   2

   Questions that ask you to *infer* something mean that you have to *work this out* from what is written in the passage rather than look for it directly. You answer might look something like this: *We can infer the writer was a good swimmer because he was good enough to compete in a 'national* championship' (1 mark). *He also seems to think that those who make the rules for competitive swimming tend to overreact when these rules are broken. This is suggested by the humorous comparison 'finishing incorrectly is treated with as much contempt as kicking sacks of kittens into a canal.'* (1 mark).

3. How does the rest of the fourth paragraph help you understand the meaning of 'dichotomy'?

   2

   To answer this question you must first work out the meaning of the word 'dichotomy' and then quote and comment on the words in the paragraph that helped you to arrive at this meaning. You might write down that *dichotomy means two opposing things* (1 mark). *This is suggested by the two contrasting expressions: 'wave of Games-inspired media goodwill' and 'coverage of us disabled types has been increasingly hostile and negative'* (1 mark).

4. '... a government keen to push its thorny agenda of welfare reform.' (line 24).

    Identify the technique the writer is using in this expression and comment on its effectiveness. **3**

    To answer this question you should focus on the word 'thorny'. Obviously an agenda can't literally be covered in thorns so the writer is using a *metaphor* (1 mark). You could then say it is an effective expression because 'thorny' suggests something that is potentially difficult (1 mark) or even painful (thorns can scratch you) (1 mark). A 'thorny problem' is an expression often used to describe something that is difficult to solve.

5. Give a brief summary of the main points the writer makes in paragraph 5. Use your own words as much as possible. **3**

    To answer this question, first of all look over paragraph 5 again. Then underline or highlight what you think the key points are (*locate*); then turn them into your own words as far as you can (*translate*). This question is a test of how well you understand the passage and of your own vocabulary.

    You might underline:

    *   The word 'scroungers' has become a tabloid staple, attached to tales of disabled people living in 18-bedroom mansions and water-skiing.
    *   the number is infinitesimally small
    *   many disabled people, myself included, have felt tarred by the same very uncomfortable brush. Benefit has become a dirty word again

    Then simply turn these points into your own words so your answer would look something like:

    *   Some newspapers publish exaggerated stories of disabled people cheating the benefits system.
    *   Very few disabled people actually do this.
    *   Lots of disabled people feel they are unfairly targeted just because they receive benefits.

    You would receive 1 mark for each part of your answer.

6. Comment on the writer's use of *language* (including *word choice* and *sentence structure*) in paragraphs 7 and 8 and go on to say what effect this achieves. **5**

    In your answer you might say that some of the writer's *word choice* is *informal* or *colloquial* in terms of style and tone ('no arms, no legs bloke'; 'down the pub'; 'not bashing the Paralympics'). Some of the sentence structure reinforces this informality. The use of *short sentences*: 'They're superhuman. They're athletes.'; 'Don't get me wrong.'; 'However, I'm not superhuman.' does this as does the *minor sentence*, 'In the non-pejorative sense of the word.' There are also lots of contractions ('They're'; 'Don't'; 'aren't'), which are also features of this type of style. You could then add that the effect of this informality is to make the reader feel the writer is talking directly to us – that we're being invited to share his experiences and thoughts on this issue.

The use of *repetition* is another obvious feature of sentence structure ('... they're different ... They're superhuman. They're athletes. They're not like me ...'). This type of repetition helps to reinforce the writer's argument.

There are also examples of a more formal style and tone in these paragraphs ('One suspects that they will be covered without any sense of irony.'; '... on the cusp of a real change...'; 'non-pejorative'). These remind us that the writer is also making a very serious point.

You would get 1 mark for each valid point you make. For each point you would have to quote or refer to a language feature and then comment on it as shown above. For full marks you would have to comment on word choice *and* sentence structure as these are the two features specified in the question.

7. What does the writer hope will be one way that the Paralympics will affect 'ordinary disabled people' (line 45)?   **1**

This is another straightforward *understanding* type question. *Locate* the answer and *translate* it into your own words. The writer says that he hopes 'that disability will be normalised' so your answer should go something like: *He hopes that being disabled is not seen as anything different or special* (1 mark).

8. Why might the reader be surprised by the final sentence of paragraph 9?   **2**

The clue here is in the word 'surprised'. You should look for anything out of the ordinary or 'odd' in the sentence. Here it seems strange that the writer doesn't want disabled people to be thought of as 'amazing and wonderful and brave', which are all very positive things that people would usually like to hear about themselves (1 mark). The surprising thing is the fact he says that this would be the 'worst thing that could happen' (1 mark).

9. Comment on the writer's use of punctuation in paragraph 9.   **2**

You should have spotted the use of the dash and the brackets. The dash introduces an explanation of what he means by 'normalised' (1 mark). The brackets contain a humorous comment '(I obviously am ...)' This is an example of *parenthesis* (1 mark).

10. How effective do you find the final paragraph as a conclusion to the article as a whole? You should refer to ideas and specific language features in your answer. **3**

You're free to say that you find the ending effective or ineffective. This question asks you to analyse the language features used by the writer and to show how they contribute to the effectiveness of the final paragraph. Any time you are asked about 'language features' you should consider such things as word choice, sentence structure, imagery, sound, etc.

It's usually easier to argue that the writing is effective. Here are some of the features that you could say make it an effective conclusion to the article (1 mark for each one you identify):

- The writer ends with a plea 'I want …'
- There's more of the humour we've seen throughout the passage 'OK, shuffle'; 'David bloody Weir'.
- The short final (minor) sentence, which adds impact to the writer's final wish.
- Positive word choice to describe the Paralympians' achievements: 'lauded'; 'talents and achievements'.
- Using sentence structure to highlight contrasting ideas 'because of those things, not in spite of their disability'.

11. What do you think the writer's purpose was in writing this article? **2**

To answer this you need to think about the passage as a whole. Ask yourself what exactly the writer is trying to achieve. The headline above the article provides a good clue. Your answer might look something like: *Paul Carter hopes the Games will make life more normal for disabled people* (1 mark), *who face increasing hostility because of changes to the benefits system* (1 mark).

12. Who do you think the intended audience is for this article? Support your answer with evidence from the passage. **2**

Think about who the writer is trying to convince. The intended audience seems to be the able-bodied general readers whose attitude to disabled people he wants to change (2 marks). Again, the headline provides the clue and there are many other things you could quote from the passage to support your answer. You would also get 1 mark for making a more basic point such as *people interested in sport* or *people interested in disability issues*.

Total 30

Practice passage

Now that you've seen how you might tackle this part of the question paper, try the practice passage that follows. It's another one on a sporting theme. You'll find answers on pages 84–86.

Friday's Local Heroes: Renicks eager to take sister act to Glasgow

Kimberley, in white, and Louise, in blue, at GB Judo's Ratho Climbing Centre headquarters on the outskirts of Edinburgh.

For the first time in an hour, silence falls upon the gym.

The conversation, until then unrelenting and candid, is curtailed as Kimberley and Louise Renicks repudiate the request to describe one another. The Coatbridge judokas exchange steely looks, each
5   silently willing the other to speak first. 'Right, I'll go,' says Kimberley, reluctantly. 'Louise is caring, mothering and bossy …' The older sister bristles ever so slightly, then deliberately delivers her verdict. 'Kimberley fights like a lion but she's so laid back, she's horizontal.'

The warm assessments harbour gentle chastisements and are indicative
10 of the maternal relationship between the pair. Only five years separate the sisters but 30-year-old Louise instinctively assumes authority, be it a consequence of her initial dominance in their contests on the mat or, more mundanely, because she collects learner driver Kimberley from the family home each day on the way from her Glasgow flat
15 to training. 'My brother and myself always want to protect her,' says Louise, referencing their middle sibling, 29-year-old Thomas. 'You don't want her to experience any bad things you may have and, anyway, the youngest always gets spoiled …'

20 Kimberley, who won't introduce boyfriends to 'scary' Louise, concedes her sister is the first person she texts whenever she gets off a plane. That bond, forged amid childhood play fights, has continued through hours of hard work, long-distance travel, fraught competition and personal turmoil and will continue to be a source of comfort as the duo attempt to confirm their participation in the Glasgow Commonwealth Games.

25 As it stands, both are expected to earn the solitary places in their respective divisions, Kimberley having moved down from the under-52kg weight category that she shared with Louise to ensure both had the opportunity to qualify. 'I could have moved up but Kimberley had a lot of puppy fat,' says Louise, grinning. 'She's always been a wee
30 ball …'

'When I went to college I learned more about nutrition and training,' explains Kimberley, who started competing at the age of six and was fighting at senior level by the age of 14. 'When I was younger, I would sneak a bar of chocolate or a packet of crisps but I started to
35 listen and the weight dropped. Then I took a medal in my first event at under-48kg and, in the second, I beat the Olympic champion and that helped convince me.'

It was, perhaps, just as well. The sisters had fought six times in competition by then, Louise having dominated the first few fights
40 before Kimberley began to wrest the initiative, but it was becoming too much of a strain. Both girls found their emotions became wrought, albeit after the fights, as the stakes increased and the repercussions of defeat grew more serious.

Louise, being older, felt it more but Kimberley admits her competitive
45 instincts were becoming compromised, too, even if it rarely showed on the mat. 'I got beat in a semi by a Cuban who nearly snapped my ankle,' Louise recalls. 'Then I had to fight Kimberley for the bronze and she kept battering the same ankle because she knew it was hurting. Once we're on the mat together, we really go at it.'

50 Judo, then, offers a release from that maternal relationship but also from the difficulties surrounding the sisters. Two years ago their mother, Agnes, was diagnosed with a brain disease that has affected her motor skills and, while she is mercifully pain-free, she requires intensive care and physiotherapy. Having managed to establish a routine, the girls
55 can now plan their training around such responsibilities but Louise initially opted to step back from the sport for six months, reckoning Kimberley had a better chance of making the Olympics, and lost her funding as a consequence.

60 Ultimately, neither made the London Games, both missing out on a place by just a few points and having to settle for reserve spots, but neither girl has room for regret. 'I needed to be there for my mum,' Louise says. 'I'm here because of her and our dad Thomas, who got us into judo and still runs a club. Now I am so determined to make the Commonwealths so she can be there and remember it before
65 dementia kicks in.'

The qualification window for Glasgow 2014 begins on May 1, just a week after the European Championship, at which the girls are expected to make an impact given they both hold world rankings in the mid-30s. Despite that, though, neither can afford to slack:
70 Kimberley because she wants a high seeding; Louise because she has been warned a bad year will result in a younger fighter being selected for development purposes instead.

A critical 18 months lie ahead, a period in which the sisters must become even more professional, more disciplined and more wary.
75 'Our coaches have told us we are classed as medal contenders,' says Louise. 'Inside you want that but, when you hear it, it's pressure. Sometimes I just want to shut myself away.

'When I do go out, though, I don't accept a drink from anyone because you don't know who might have spiked it and we get tested
80 every week. If I put my drink down to dance, I don't finish it and it's even taken me two-and-a-half years to let my partner get me one.'

Then there are the chancers and the bams; guys with a drink in them who want to challenge the judokas to a fight. Kimberley often uses her diminutive figure to deny her status but Louise, ever the protector,
85 is less circumspect. 'Sometimes people look at you as a trophy,' she explains. 'I've had drunken men think they are funny and tried to choke me from behind. Big guys. And I'm thinking 'whit are ye daen?' and the rage comes. I've seen me throw people over tables …'

'Aye, flip guys over in front of their friends, even though we're only
90 eight stone,' adds Kimberley, grinning, before Louise continues. 'We went to a school to do a talk last week and there were a few neddy boys saying to Kimberley 'Ah'll take ye on' and I was thinking 'aye, okay then, I dare ye'.'

The anecdote is delivered deadpan, the maternal instinct kicking in again. 'Told you,' Kimberley says, smiling.

Adapted from an article by Richard Winton in *The Herald*, 15 March 2013

Questions

		Marks
1.	Read the first paragraph. **In your own words**, describe the change that takes place in the conversation between the writer and the Renicks sisters.	2
2.	Look at lines 10–15. **In your own words**, explain why Louise 'instinctively assumes authority' over her younger sister.	3
3.	Look at lines 26–61. **In your own words**, explain the difficulties Kimberley has had to overcome in her judo career.	4
4.	Explain how the writer's use of sentence structure helps to clarify the information conveyed to the reader in lines 66–74. You should refer to two examples in your answer.	4
5.	Look at lines 78–81. **In your words**, explain what Louise tells the writer about in this paragraph.	3
6.	Look at lines 82–88. In your own words, explain the different ways the sisters respond when challenged by 'guys with a drink in them'.	4
7.	What do you think the use of Scots words adds to this article? You should refer to specific examples in your answer.	4
8.	Choose one of the following images: • 'exchange steely looks' (line 4) • 'bristles ever so slightly' (line 7) • 'look at you as a trophy' (line 85) Explain what your chosen image means and analyse its effect.	3
9.	Identify the writer's attitude to the Renicks sisters in this article and give two pieces of evidence to support your answer.	3
	Total	**30**

How to deal with the questions on Scottish texts

This part of the National 5 exam is designed to test your ability to understand, analyse and evaluate an extract taken from one of the Scottish set texts.

Exactly what you study will very much depend on the decisions made by the English teachers at your school but you will probably study at least two of the set texts (or look at all the poems for your chosen poet) during your National 5 course. This will allow you to choose between at least two questions in the exam. You can also use a Scottish text as the subject of your critical essay (see the table on page 56) but not the one printed in the exam.

This part of the exam is worth 20 marks in total and the questions will be worth 1–8 marks each. You will be asked questions about the extract printed in the exam paper and about your wider knowledge of the text(s).

This part of the exam will last for 45 minutes.

On the following pages you will find a selection of questions on Scottish texts for practice.

The SQA intends to refresh this list every few years. For the first years of this exam, the Scottish set texts are as follows:

Drama
Bold Girls by Rona Munro

Sailmaker by Alan Spence

Tally's Blood by Ann Marie di Mambro

Prose
Various short stories by Iain Crichton Smith
- 'The Red Door'
- 'The Telegram'
- 'Mother and Son'
- 'In Church'
- 'The Painter'
- 'The Crater'

Hieroglyphics and Other Stories by Anne Donovan
- 'All that Glisters'
- 'Zimmerobics'
- 'Virtual Pals'
- 'Away in a Manger'

- 'A Chitterin' Bite'
- 'Dear Santa'

The Testament of Gideon Mack by James Robertson

Kidnapped by Robert Louis Stevenson

The Cone Gatherers by Robin Jenkins

Poetry

Carol Ann Duffy

- 'War Photographer'
- 'Havisham'
- 'Valentine'
- 'Originally'
- 'Anne Hathaway'
- 'Mrs Midas'

Norman MacCaig

- 'Sounds of the Day'
- 'Assisi'
- 'Visiting Hour'
- 'Memorial'
- 'Aunt Julia'
- 'Basking Shark'

Edwin Morgan

- 'In the Snack Bar'
- 'Trio'
- 'Hyena'
- 'Good Friday'
- 'Winter'
- 'Slate'

Jackie Kay

- 'My Grandmother's Houses'
- 'Lucozade'
- 'Gap Year'
- 'Bed'
- 'Divorce'
- 'Keeping Orchids'

Bold Girls, by Rona Munro

Read the extract printed below and then answer the questions that follow.
See pages 86–87 for the answers

Photograph of the New Venture Theatre's 2009 production of Bold Girls (Strat Mastoris/NVT)

> *Nora and Cassie fall silent.*
> *Marie goes to the kitchen area, opens some crisps, puts them in a bowl, brings them out and sets them down.*
> *Nora and Cassie stare at their drinks.*
>
> 5 **CASSIE** I never hated you.
> *Nora scrubs one fierce hand over her eyes but gives no sign she's heard.*
> I just wanted you to make it happen different.
> **NORA** Well you'll need to go to some other place where they make the world different, Cassie.
> 10 **CASSIE** Well so I will.
> **NORA** You do that.
> **CASSIE** I will. I'm leaving.
> **NORA** Though it seems to me there's not a place in the world that is different.
> 15 **CASSIE** Well I'll write and tell you.
> **NORA** Oh she's got her flight booked, Marie.
> **CASSIE** Tell her, Marie.
> **MARIE** It's not for me to tell her, Cassie.
> **CASSIE** Mummy, I've two hundred pounds saved and I'm getting out.
> 20 **NORA** Oh.

No one says anything else for a second.

NORA So you've got yourself a flat?

CASSIE No. I'm leaving Belfast.

NORA What?

25 **CASSIE** I'm getting on a ferry and I'm getting out.

NORA What are you saying to me, Cassie?

CASSIE How many ways do you want me to say it!

There is a pause.

NORA Well, where are you going?

30 **CASSIE** I'll see where I get to. I'm telling you though I'm not going to be one of those that go out on one boat and home on the next with their luck all spent. I'm leaving, Mummy.

NORA And what about your children?

CASSIE They'll be better off out of here.

35 **NORA** Are you going to just tear them out by the roots and drag them along after you?

CASSIE No... I...

NORA To live God knows where on two hundred pound?

CASSIE I'll send for them... (*Catching Marie's eye*) Oh don't look at
40 me Marie.

NORA Oh don't come it with your tall tales again, Cassie. Two hundred pounds indeed.

CASSIE Oh is it proof you're wanting? Here then. (*She gets up and goes to Michael's picture.*)

45 **MARIE** Cassie what are you doing?

Cassie feels behind it, stops then starts running her hand frantically over the back of the picture.

What are you doing to Michael?

Cassie pulls it off the wall and looks at the back of it. She stares at it
50 *for a minute then turns to Marie.*

CASSIE Where is it?

MARIE What?

CASSIE My money. Where'd you put it Marie?

MARIE I never touched a penny of yours, Cassie!

55 **CASSIE** You were the only one knew I had it.

MARIE I never knew you'd hidden it up the back of Michael!

CASSIE I had to put it through here; have you seen the way she dusts? (*She points at Nora.*)

MARIE Well I never touched your money, Cassie.

60 **CASSIE** Oh Jesus, someone's lifted it. (*She collapses back into her chair, still clutching Michael's picture.*) They've taken my money off me! (*She bows her head. She seems about to cry.*)

Nora and Marie look at each other.

NORA (*Crossing to her*) Cassie?

65 *Cassie shakes her head.*

(*Hesitating a moment*)

Och you're not crying, are you?

Cassie just looks at her.

Well, what age are you to be making up daydreams and
70 spoiling your face crying for them. Come on, now.

Nora pats briskly at Cassie's shoulder.

Cassie knocks Nora's hand away.

Well you're not going anywhere, Cassie Ryan. That's clear as
daylight.

75 **CASSIE** (*Quietly*) I'm going anyway, money or no money.

NORA But your home's here! Your family's here!

CASSIE Yes. It is.

Cassie and Nora stare at each other for a few seconds.

NORA And what I feel goes for nothing, does it?

80 **CASSIE** What do you feel, Mummy? For me? What have you got left?

Nora turns away from her, shaking.

*Marie takes a step towards her but before she can get there Nora turns,
struggling to look right.*

NORA Well – thanks for the sandwich Marie, but we'll not be
85 troubling you further; you must be desperate for your bed.

CASSIE (*Still staring at Nora*) Can I get another drink, Marie?

Marie hesitates again, looking between them.

NORA (*Pleading*) Cassie...

CASSIE Good-night, Mummy. (*She looks away from Nora.*)

90 **NORA** (*Drawing herself up*) Oh you'll be telling me a different tale
in the morning! There's no end to your wild tales, Cassie!
There's no end to them, Marie!

(*She snatches up her drink and takes an angry gulp.*)

And I'd it all to do. I'd it all to put up with! Are you hearing me?

95 *Cassie doesn't look at Nora.*

(*Taking another gulp.*)

He's lost my remnant, Marie. He's lost it. I'd all the money
saved, as good as paid. It's gone he says, gone. I'll never
find a colour like that again. Months I'd been dreaming of
100 the glow that would give my front room. Months. And he's
lost it. I'll never have it the way I want it now. Never. (*She is
getting tearful in her turn.*) My lovely wee room. It could be
lovely, couldn't it, Marie?

MARIE You'll get it right, Nora.

105 **NORA**   Well where will I ever find a colour like that again? Tell me
                that? (*Waiting for a response*) Cassie? I'm asking you!

   CASSIE   (*Looking up at Nora*) Good-night, Mummy.

   Nora stares at her for a moment, then she nods.

   NORA   Well I'm going up the town tomorrow. I'm just going to go
110   up the town and buy a piece of what I want. I'll get credit.
               I'll give them a false address and I'll get credit and I'll have
               my loose covers. And if you don't want to come and help
               choose them, Cassie, you needn't sit on them.

   Nora exits.

115 *Marie puts the gin bottle down in front of Cassie. Cassie helps herself
    to another drink.*

   MARIE   (*Quietly*) It'll tear the heart out of her, Cassie.

   CASSIE   Mummy's heart is made of steel. She had to grow it that way.

   Marie reaches over and takes Michael's picture. She goes and rehangs
120 *it carefully.*

Questions

1. In what ways are Marie's actions in the stage direction in line 2 typical
    of this character?   1

2. 'Though it seems to me there's not a place in the world that is different'
    (lines 13–14). What does this suggest about Nora's view of life?   1

3. What is the effect of the stage direction in line 21 'No one says
    anything else for a second'?   2

4. Comment on the word choice and imagery of Nora's line 'tear them
    out by the roots and drag them along after you'.   2

5. What sort of look do you think Marie gives Cassie in line 39?   1

6. Why might it be considered ironic that Cassie chose to hide the money
    behind the picture of Michael?   2

7. What do lines 109–118 suggest about Nora? Support your answer with
    evidence from the text.   3

8. This extract illustrates the theme of broken dreams in the play. Choose
    another theme that is explored in the play and briefly describe how
    Rona Munro presents it to the audience.   8

                                                            Total   20

'The Telegram', by Iain Crichton Smith

Read the extract printed below and then answer the questions that follow. See pages 88–89 for the answers.

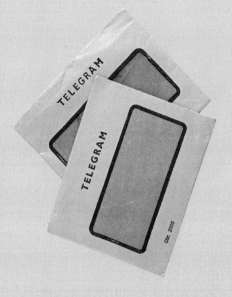

The two women — one fat and one thin — sat at the window of the thin woman's house drinking tea and looking down the road which ran through the village. They were like two birds, one a fat domestic bird perhaps, the other more aquiline, more gaunt, or, to be precise,
5   more like a buzzard.

It was wartime and though the village appeared quiet, much had gone on in it. Reverberations from a war fought far away had reached it: many of its young men had been killed, or rather drowned, since nearly all of them had joined the Navy, and their ships had sunk in
10   seas which they had never seen except on maps which hung on the walls of the local school which they all had at one time or another unwillingly attended. One had been drowned on a destroyer after a leave during which he had told his family that he would never come back again. (Or at least that was the rumour in the village which
15   was still, as it had always been, a superstitious place.) Another had been drowned during the pursuit of the *Bismarck*.

What the war had to do with them the people of the village did not know. It came on them as a strange plague, taking their sons away and then killing them, meaninglessly, randomly. They watched the
20   road often for the telegrams.

The telegrams were brought to the houses by the local elder who, clad in black, would walk along the road and then stop at the house

25 to which the telegram was directed. People began to think of the telegram as a strange missile pointed at them from abroad. They did not know what to associate it with, certainly not with God, but it was a weapon of some kind, it picked a door and entered it, and left desolation just like any other weapon.

The two women who watched the street were different, not only physically but socially. For the thin woman's son was a sub-
30 lieutenant in the Navy while the fat woman's son was only an ordinary seaman. The fat woman's son had to salute the thin woman's son. One got more pay than the other, and wore better uniform. One had been at university and had therefore become an officer, the other had left school at the age of fourteen.

35 When they looked out the window they could see cows wandering lazily about, but little other movement. The fat woman's cow used to eat the thin woman's washing and she was looking out for it but she couldn't see it. The thin woman was not popular in the village. She was an incomer from another village and had only been in this
40 one for thirty years or so. The fat woman had lived in the village all her days; she was a native. Also the thin woman was ambitious: she had sent her son to university though she only had a widow's pension of ten shillings a week.

As they watched they could see at the far end of the street the tall
45 man in black clothes carrying in his hand a piece of yellow paper. This was a bare village with little colour and therefore the yellow was both strange and unnatural.

The fat woman said: 'It's Macleod again.'

'I wonder where he's going today.'

50 They were both frightened for he could be coming to their house. And so they watched him and as they watched him they spoke feverishly as if by speaking continually and watching his every move they would be able to keep from themselves whatever plague he was bringing. The thin woman said:

55 'Don't worry, Sarah, it won't be for you. Donald only left home last week.'

'You don't know,' said the fat woman, 'you don't know.' And then she added without thinking, 'It's different for the officers.'

'Why is it different for the officers?' said the thin woman in an even
60 voice without taking her eyes from the black figure.

'Well, I just thought they're better off,' said the fat woman in a confused tone, 'they get better food and they get better conditions.'

65   'They're still on the ship,' said the thin woman who was thinking that the fat woman was very stupid. But then most of them were: they were large, fat and lazy. Most of them could have better afforded to send their sons and daughters to university but they didn't want to be thought of as snobbish.

70   'They are that,' said the fat woman. 'But your son is educated,' she added irrelevantly. Of course her son didn't salute the thin woman's son if they were both home on leave at the same time. It had happened once they had been. But naturally there was the uneasiness.

75   'I made sacrifices to have my son educated,' said the thin woman. 'I lived on a pension of ten shillings a week. I was in nobody's debt. More tea?'

'No thank you,' said the fat woman. 'He's passed Bessie's house. That means it can't be Roddy. He's safe.'

80   For a terrible moment she realised that she had hoped that the elder would have turned in at Bessie's house. Not that she had anything against Bessie or Roddy. But still one thought of one's own family first.

85   The thin woman continued remorselessly as if she were pecking away at something she had pecked at for many years. 'The teacher told me to send Iain to University. He came to see me. I had no thought of sending him before he came. 'Send your son to university,' he said to me. 'He's got a good head on him.' And I'll tell you, Sarah, I had to save every penny. Ten shillings isn't much. When did you see me with good clothes in the church?'

90   'That's true,' said the fat woman absently. 'We have to make sacrifices.'

Questions

1. What does the imagery used to describe the two women in paragraph 1 (lines 3–5) suggest about their appearance and personalities?   **2**

2. Identify the technique the writer uses to describe the war in paragraph 3 (lines 18–19) and comment on its effectiveness.   **3**

3. Which word, used later in the passage, continues the idea contained in 'plague'?   **1**

4. '… the village which was still, as it had always been, a superstitious place.' (paragraph 2)

    How does the women's behaviour later in this extract illustrate the superstitious nature of the villagers?   **1**

5. What is surprising about the description of the thin woman as 'an incomer'?   2

6. What does this description of the thin woman suggest about the village where the story is set?   2

7. What can you infer about the thin woman's lifestyle from the information in this extract?   1

8. Show how the use of setting in this short story is similar or different to another short story by Iain Crichton Smith that you have studied.   8

Total   20

'All that Glisters', by Anne Donovan

Read the extract printed below and then answer the questions that follow.
See pages 89–90 for the answers.

Thon wee wifie brung them in, the wan that took us for two days
when Mrs McDonald wis aff. She got us tae make Christmas cards wi
coloured cardboard and felties, which is a bit much when we're in
second year, but naebdy wis gonnae say anythin cos it's better than
5   daein real work. Anyway ah like daein things like that and made a
right neat wee card for ma daddy wi a Christmas tree and a robin
and a bit a holly on it.

That's lovely, dear. What's your name?
Clare.
10   *Would you like to use the glitter pens?*
And she pulled oot the pack fae her bag.

Ah'd never seen them afore. When ah wis in primary four the
teacher gied us tubes of glitter but it wis quite messy. Hauf the stuff
ended up on the flair and it wis hard tae make sure you got the
15   glue in the right places. But these pens were different cos the glue
wis mixed in wi the glitter so you could jist draw with them. It wis
pure brilliant, so it wis. There wis four colours, rid, green, gold and
silver, and it took a wee while tae get the hang of it. You had tae be
careful when you squeezed the tube so's you didnae get a big blob
20   appearin at wanst, but efter a few goes ah wis up an runnin.

And when ah'd finished somethin amazin hud happened. Ah
cannae explain whit it wis but the glitter jist brought everythin tae
life, gleamin and glisterin agin the flat cardboard. It wis like the
difference between a Christmas tree skinklin wi fairy lights an wan
25   lyin deid an daurk in a corner.

Ma daddy wis dead chuffed. He pit the card on the bedside table and smiled. *Fair brightens up this room, hen.*

It's good tae find sumpn that cheers him up even a wee bit because ma daddy's really sick. He's had a cough fur as long as ah can remember, and
30   he husny worked fur years, but these past three month he cannae even get oot his bed. Ah hear him coughin in the night sometimes and it's different fae the way he used tae cough, comes fae deeper inside him somehow, seems tae rack his hale body fae inside oot. When ah come in fae school ah go and sit wi him and tell him aboot whit's happened that day, but hauf the time he
35   looks away fae me and stares at a patch on the downie cover where there's a coffee stain that ma ma cannae wash oot. He used tae work strippin oot buildins and he wis breathin in stour aw day, sometimes it wis that bad he'd come hame wi his hair and his claes clartit wi it. He used tae kid on he wis a ghost and walk in the hoose wi his airms stretched oot afore him and ah'd
40   rin and hide unner the stair, watchin him walk by wi the faint powdery white ness floatin roon his heid.

He never knew there wis asbestos in the dust, never knew a thing aboot it then, nane of them did. Noo he's an expert on it, read up aw these books tae try and unnerstaun it fur the compensation case. Before he got really
45   sick he used tae talk aboot it sometimes.

You see, hen, the word asbestos comes fae a Greek word that means indestructible. That's how they use it fur fireproofin — the fire cannae destroy it.

You mean if you wore an asbestos suit you could walk through fire and it
50   *widnae hurt you?*

Aye. In the aulden days they used tae bury the royals in it. They cried it the funeral dress of kings.

Questions
1. Using your own words, describe the narrator's reaction to being asked 'tae make Christmas cards wi coloured cardboard and felties'? **2**
2. (a) What is the difference between the language used by the supply teacher and the language used by Clare? **1**

   (b) Why do you think Anne Donovan has chosen to show this difference? **2**
3. Clare describes the glitter pens ('rid, green, gold and silver'). Why is the reference to colour an important feature of this extract? **2**
4. What does the reader learn about Clare's father in lines 23–45? Use your own words in your answer. **2**
5. (a) Why might Clare's father's statement 'They cried it the funeral dress of kings' (lines 51–52) be considered ironic? **2**

   (b) Identify and comment on another example of irony from the extract. **1**
6. Show how the language and ideas of this short story are similar or different to another short story by Anne Donovan you have read. **8**

Total 20

'Originally', by Carol Ann Duffy

Read this poem carefully and then answer the questions that follow.

We came from our own country in a red room
which fell through the fields, our mother singing
our father's name to the turn of the wheels.
My brothers cried, one of them bawling *Home,*
5   *Home,* as the miles rushed back to the city,
the street, the house, the vacant rooms
where we didn't live any more. I stared
at the eyes of a blind toy, holding its paw.

All childhood is an emigration. Some are slow,
10   leaving you standing, resigned, up an avenue
where no one you know stays. Others are sudden.
Your accent wrong. Corners, which seem familiar,
leading to unimagined, pebble-dashed estates, big boys
eating worms and shouting words you don't understand.
15   My parents' anxiety stirred like a loose tooth
in my head. *I want our own country,* I said.

> But then you forget, or don't recall, or change,
> and, seeing your brother swallow a slug, feel only
> a skelf of shame. I remember my tongue
> 20 shedding its skin like a snake, my voice
> in the classroom sounding just like the rest. Do I only think
> I lost a river, culture, speech, sense of first space
> and the right place? Now, *Where do you come from?*
> strangers ask. *Originally?* And I hesitate.

1. How does the poet's language convey contrasting moods in the first stanza? **3**

2. 'All childhood is an emigration.' (line 9). What do you think the poet means by this? **2**

3. 'My parents' anxiety stirred like a loose tooth in my head.' (lines 15–16). Why is this an effective and appropriate simile to use in this context? **2**

4. '... feel only a skelf of shame.' (lines 18–19). Why is this an effective and appropriate metaphor to use in this context? **2**

5. 'I remember my tongue/shedding its skin like a snake' (lines 19–20). Why is this an effective and appropriate image to use in this context? **2**

6. Why does the speaker 'hesitate' in the final line of the poem? **1**

7. Is the use of imagery in this poem similar or different to its use in another poem by Carol Ann Duffy that you have read? **8**

Total 20

The Cone-Gatherers, by Robin Jenkins

Read the extract printed below and then answer the questions that follow. See pages 92–94 for the answers.

As she ran, and stumbled, climbed fences, jumped over streams, scrambled up banks, and plunged deep into leaves, Lady Runcie-Campbell tried to make her anger against the cone gatherers grow.
Their insolence, independence and their even more outrageous
5   attempt at revenge, resulting in the prolonged danger to her son, were surely just reasons for hating and despising them; for wishing Duror well in his intention to chastise them into decency and obedience; and for vowing, when all this was over, to obliterate the forester's false yellow smile of comprehension and forgiveness by
10   complaining to his superiors so strongly that they must either dismiss him or degrade him. As a mother, as a landowner, as a Christian even, surely she was justified? Yet not for a second of that dreadful journey to the Point did she convince herself. Whatever she ought to feel, anger seemed wrong and unavailing. She kept remembering
15   Roderick's strange chatter that morning about Bhudda; Harry after she'd struck him, and also before he had, trembling with shyness and trepidation, offered to climb the tree; Duror with the naked doll in his fist and the obscene accusations so lusciously on his lips; old Graham at the fir tree stinking so rankly of sweat and whispering
20   so compassionately into her ear; and always, dominating every other memory, the two cone gatherers leaving the beach hut. Fear, anxiety, love, sorrow, regret, and hope, were in her mind, but not anger.

From the silver fir to the Point took ten minutes; during them she
25   seemed to travel to the furthest limits of her being, there to be baulked by not finding what she had hoped to find, and without which she could never return.

Behind her, always at that proper distance, ran Baird, a big red-eared solemn man, who kept thinking what a good thing it was he had,
30   after all, taken Manson with him to the tree. The lady had promised to reward Bob; but it was a recognised rule of the world that if a subordinate was rewarded, his master must be rewarded also, to maintain stations, and of course more handsomely according to his higher degree. In the war, for instance, there were different medals
35   for privates and officers, although they fought in the same battles.

From a bank of whins and bracken she looked down on the promontory. Never had the loch been so potently beautiful: it was as vast, bright,

40 and detailed as in a dream; and there seemed to be a wonderful interpretation, if it could only be known. A warship steamed down the loch. So intimate a part of the dream was it, she seemed, during those few moments of suspense upon the bank, to know all its crew and what was to be each man's fate in the sea towards which it was bound. There, too, dream-like, were the pines, her favourite trees, making against sea and sky what had always struck her as Scottish gestures,
45 recalling the eerie tormented tragic grandeur of the old native ballads. Gulls, as prodigal of time and sky as she must be parsimonious, flew and shrieked high over them.

She could not see any men; they must be hidden by the trees. But as she began to go down the bank, tearing her clothes on the whins
50 and splintering the bracken, she heard the report of a gun, followed by a scream, and then by the quickened wails of the gulls.

As she raced among the pines, making for that gunshot, she prayed that Duror in his madness had not hurt the cone gatherers, not for their sakes, nor for his, nor for his wife's, but for her son's.

55 She saw Duror before she saw them. He was walking away among the pine trees with so infinite a desolation in his every step that it was this memory of him, rather than that of the little hunchback dangling from the tree, or that of his brother climbing so frenziedly up into it, which was to torment her sleep for months.

60 She forced herself to go over to the tree. It was the strap of his bag which had caught on a branch. He hung therefore in twisted fashion, and kept swinging. His arms were loose and dangled in macabre gestures of supplication. Though he smiled, he was dead. From his bag dropped a cone, and then another. There might
65 have been more, but other drops, also singly, but faster and faster, distracted her: these were of blood.

With moans and yelps of lamentation like an animal his brother was struggling along that branch to try and reach him.

As she watched, with Baird as horrified as she, another gunshot rang
70 out. She glanced at him and saw that it had not occurred to him so soon what it meant. She knew that somewhere, on her beloved promontory, Duror, with his face shattered and bloody, lay dead.

Then, while she stood there emptied by horror, she heard far away a voice she loved screaming in excitement: 'Mother, he's down. It's
75 all right. He's safe. Harry got him down.'

80 Baird thought she had not heard. Not looking at the cone-gatherer still trying to reach his dead brother, and not daring to approach too close to her, he took a step forward and told her what Sheila was still screaming.

85 What she did then shocked him, even there amidst those shocking sights.

First she said: 'Help him, Baird.' Then she went down on her knees, near the blood and the spilt cones. She could not pray, but she could weep; and as she wept pity, and purified hope, and joy,

90 welled up in her heart.

1. How does the language of paragraph 1 (lines 1–23) help to suggest Lady Runcie-Campbell's state of mind at this point in the novel? **3**

2. Briefly describe the events that have led up to this point in the narrative. **2**

3. How does the third paragraph (lines 28–35) help to illustrate an important theme of the novel? **2**

4. Why do you think Jenkins includes the reference to the warship in line 39? **2**

5. '… with so infinite a desolation in his every step' (line 56). How effective do you find this image used to describe Duror? **2**

6. 'She could not pray, but she could weep; and as she wept pity, and purified hope, and joy, welled up in her heart.' (lines 88–90) Why does Lady Runcie-Campbell react in this way? **1**

7. Calum is often described as a 'Christ-like' character. How does Jenkins suggest this to the reader? You should support your answer by referring to the extract and to the rest of the novel. **8**

Total 20

'Sounds of the Day', by Norman MacCaig

Read this poem carefully and then answer the questions that follow.
See pages 94–95 for the answers.

> When a clatter came,
> It was horses crossing the ford.
> When the air creaked, it was
> A lapwing seeing us off the premises
> 5 Of its private marsh. A snuffling puff
> Ten yards from the boat was the tide blocking,
> Unblocking a hole in a rock.
> When the black drums rolled, it was water
> Falling sixty feet into itself.
>
> 10 When the door
> Scraped shut, it was the end
> Of all the sounds there are.
>
> You left me
> Beside the quietest fire in the world.
>
> 15 I thought I was hurt in my pride only,
> Forgetting that,
> When you plunge your hand in freezing water,
> You feel
> A bangle of ice around your wrist
> 20 Before the whole hand goes numb.

Questions

1. Comment on the poet's use of sound in stanza 1 and stanza 2.   **4**

2. How does MacCaig suggest the significance of the third stanza?   **2**

3. How does MacCaig use sentence structure to good effect in this poem?   **4**

4. How effective do you find MacCaig's use of imagery in the final stanza?   **2**

5. Show how the treatment of the theme of loss in this poem is similar or
    different to its treatment in another poem by MacCaig you have read.   **8**

                                                                                          Total   20

The critical essay

Once you've got the first element of the SQA exam out of the way, it's time for the **critical reading** paper. Section 2 of the critical reading paper requires you to write a critical essay.

Key points

- The critical essay tests your skills in understanding, evaluation and analysis.
- You will write **ONE** critical essay on a text you have studied as part of your course.
- You will be expected to complete the essay in around 45 minutes.
- Your essay is marked out of 20.
- Your essay can be on a drama, prose, poetry, film and TV drama text or on a language topic.
- Each of these genres will have two questions to choose from.
- Your choice of critical essay question will also depend on which Scottish text you are going to answer on. You cannot use the same genre for both section 1 and section 2 of the question paper.

Questions on Scottish texts	Critical essay
If you answer on:	Your critical essay must be on:
Drama: • *Bold Girls*, or • *Sailmaker*, or • *Tally's Blood*	• A prose text, or • A poem, or • A film or TV drama, or • A language topic
Prose: • Iain Crichton Smith short stories, or • Anne Donovan short stories, or • *The Testament of Gideon Mack*, or • *Kidnapped*, or • *The Cone-Gatherers*	• A drama text, or • A poem, or • A film or TV drama, or • A language topic
Poetry: • Carol Ann Duffy, or • Edwin Morgan, or • Norman MacCaig, or • Jackie Kay	• A drama text, or, • A prose text, or • A film or TV drama, or • A language topic

Let's look at how your essay will be marked. Your marker will allocate your essay to one of five categories and then decide on a final mark within that category. The table on the next page shows what the features of a **very good** essay are (Category 1) and the features of an essay that is **just good enough to pass** (Category 3).

	Category 1 Essays in this category will be awarded 20, 19 or 18 marks.	Category 3 Essays in this category will be awarded 13, 12, 11 or 10 marks.
The candidate demonstrates:	• a **high degree of familiarity** with the text as a whole • **very good understanding** of the central concerns of the text • a line of thought which is **consistently relevant** to the task	• **some familiarity** with the text as a whole • **some understanding** of the central concerns of the text • a line of thought which is **mostly relevant** to the task
Analysis of the text demonstrates:	• **very sound awareness** of the writer's techniques through analysis, making confident use of critical terminology • **very detailed/thoughtful** explanation of stylistic devices supported by a **range of well-chosen** references and/or quotations	• an **awareness** of the writer's techniques through analysis, making some use of critical terminology • explanation of stylistic devices supported by **some appropriate** reference and/or quotation
Evaluation of the text is shown through:	• a **very well-developed** commentary of what has been enjoyed/gained from the text(s), supported by a **range of** well-chosen references to its **relevant** features	• **some** commentary of what has been enjoyed/gained from the text(s), supported by **some appropriate** reference to its features
The candidate:	• uses language to communicate a line of thought **very clearly** • uses grammar, sentence construction and punctuation which are mostly accurate • structures the essay **effectively to enhance** meaning/purpose • uses paragraphing which is **accurate and effective**	• uses language to communicate a line of thought **at first reading** • uses spelling, grammar, sentence construction and punctuation which are **mainly accurate** • attempts to structure the essay **in an appropriate way** • uses paragraphing which is **mainly accurate**
In summary, the candidate's essay is:	• thorough and precise (very good)	• fairly detailed and relevant (satisfactory)

SQA 2012

Make sure that you understand exactly what some of the terms used in the table mean.

- **Central concerns of the text** – These are the main ideas the writer is trying to communicate to the reader.
- **Line of thought** – This means that the points you make in your essay are structured in a clear, relevant and logical fashion.
- **Critical terminology** – You must be able to make confident use of the technical terms appropriate to the genre of the text you are writing about.
  - For **drama** these include: characterisation, setting, language, key incident(s), climax/turning point, plot, structure, narrative technique, theme, ideas, description …
  - For **prose** these include: characterisation, setting, language, key incident(s), climax/turning point, plot, structure, narrative technique, theme, ideas, description …
  - For **poetry** these include: word choice, tone, imagery, structure, content, rhythm, theme, sound, ideas …
  - For **film and TV drama** these include: use of camera, key sequence, characterisation, *mise-en-scène*, editing, setting, music/sound, effects, plot, dialogue …
  - For **language** these include: register, accent, dialect, slang, jargon, vocabulary, tone, abbreviation …

Once you have decided which critical essay question you are going to answer, you must be certain exactly what it is you are being asked to do. Look at this example:

> Choose a play that contains a strong female character.
>
> Briefly describe the character's role in the play and go on to explain how her strength is revealed to the audience.

Your first task is to highlight or underline the key words in the question. Remember you can mark-up the exam paper in any way you find helpful. For example:

> Choose a play that contains a strong female character.
>
> Briefly describe the character's role in the play and go on to explain how her strength is revealed to the audience.

Notice that you are being asked to do **two** things in this essay. Your answer **must** deal with both. In this case you are asked to (briefly) describe what the character does in the play and – the more substantial part of the answer – explain the various ways the playwright shows the character's strength to the reader.

Your second task is to write the plan for the essay. You can use bullet points …

* idea #1
* idea #2
* idea #3

… or a mind-map (spider diagram).

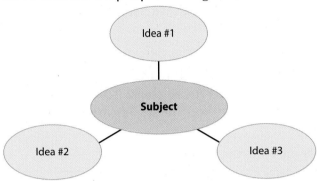

You can use whatever system works best for you.

A plan for our strong female character essay might look like this:

Play: *Bold Girls*

Strong female character: Nora

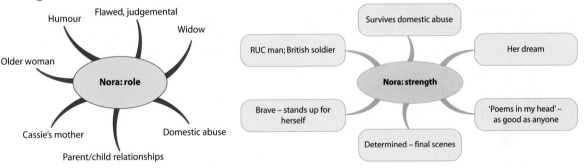

You have 45 minutes to complete the essay so spend about 5 minutes on planning and the remaining 40 on writing and checking. Always give your essay a final read over just before time is up.

5 mins Planning → 37 mins Writing and checking → 3 mins Final check

The opening paragraph of your essay should refer to the title of the text you are writing about, the author's name and the task itself (remember **T.A.T.**: title, author, task).

> **EXAM TIP**
>
> When writing the opening paragraph of your essay, remember T.A.T.: title, author, task.

Each following paragraph should develop the line of thought in your essay. The ideas you have written down in your plan will provide the content for each of these paragraphs.

Remember, each paragraph should have a **topic sentence**, which introduces, highlights or sums up what the paragraph is about. You should provide evidence – a **quotation from** or a **reference to** something in the text – to support the points you make and also explain how this evidence contributes to your argument or line of thought. If it helps, you can think of **P.E.E.** (or point, evidence, explanation) as you write. You can even use this structure multiple times within each section or paragraph. But be careful not to overdo this; the *best* essays don't read as if they've been written using a formula.

While you are being taught each text as part of your course you must revise and learn the main ideas (central concerns), the techniques used by the writer and a selection of appropriate quotations. You must be able to recall these from memory in the exam hall. Do whatever it takes to keep these in your head. In order to remember quotations:

- <u>underline</u> or highlight appropriate lines in your copy of the text
- choose relevant quotes that can be used in a variety of essays, for example quotes that illustrate theme *and* characterisation
- write quotations on sticky notes and put these where you'll keep seeing them
- put them in your phone (but don't take this into the exam hall)
- test yourself regularly.

It is important that you **link** the sections and paragraphs together effectively. Use expressions such as:

- For example
- Because of this…
- As a result … therefore
- In spite of this …
- Firstly … secondly … thirdly
- Yet … but …
- Furthermore …
- On the other hand…
- In conclusion … or To sum up …

Your final paragraph should provide an effective conclusion to your essay. In it you should sum up the points you have made and refer again to the key words of the question. This acts as a reminder to your marker that you have written a relevant response. It is vital that you keep to the question you have been set and don't just write down everything you know about a particular text.

Exemplar critical essay

Let's look at how to put all the advice given before into practice. Having thought about and planned your response, here's what the completed essay would look like.

> Choose a play that contains a strong female character.
>
> Briefly describe the character's role in the play and go on to explain how her strength is revealed to the audience.

Your opening paragraph should mention the title and author of your chosen text and refer to the question.

'Bold Girls' by Rona Munro is a play that contains a strong female character. Nora, one of the 'Bold Girls' in the play, is a woman who has managed to survive and keep going despite her personal life being affected by domestic abuse and her family life being disrupted by The Troubles in Northern Ireland in the 1970s and 80s.

Nora is older than the other three women in the play. She is Cassie's mother and a widow with a son who is in prison, presumably for terrorist offences. Rona Munro uses the character to add humour to the play; to explore the theme of parent and child relationships and to illustrate the theme of domestic violence.

A brief description of the character and her role in the play.

In many ways, Nora is a flawed character. She can be quick to judge and is sometimes very cynical. When Deirdre first arrives at Marie's house, Nora thinks she is a glue-sniffer. She also describes the girl, who is probably the mother of her son, Martin's child, as 'nothing but a wee hoor'. She has a difficult relationship with her daughter, Cassie and always seems to compare her unfavourably with her brother Martin: 'Our Martin never grudged me a cigarette'. Cassie acknowledges this when she tells Marie 'I fell out with my mummy on the delivery room floor'.

Effective use of quotation to back up the point made.

Despite these flaws, Rona Munro shows the audience that Nora is also a strong character. This is shown in the two of the anecdotes she tells in the play. In one she describes how she stood up to the RUC man who came to arrest Cassie's husband, Joe:

Effective link sentence to move the essay forward.

'And he says "And who are you?" And I says, "I'm that boy's mother-in-law, before you take him you'll have to answer to me!"

The audience laughs along with Nora and the other bold girls when she tells of how he then 'knocked her straight through the hedge'. Later in scene two at the Club, she describes how one of the Brits who had

Reference to Rona Munro's use of humour.

destroyed her bamboo suite 'with boots like anvils' assaulted her with the result that she had her ribs 'taped up for months'. She has also suffered at the hands of her husband:

'She'd come down in the morning, Marie, and find me crying on the floor with the bruises going black on my face and all she'd say was, 'Have you been upsetting daddy again?' Go and fix herself a cup of tea.'

Longer quotation placed in a separate paragraph.

These lines also show how Rona Munro suggests the relationship between fathers and daughters is different to that between mothers and daughters.

More evidence to support the idea of Nora as a strong character.

We are also shown Nora as a strong character when she refuses to give up on her dream of decorating her 'front room' just the way she wants it. The playwright uses Nora's obsession with decorating her house as a symbol of one woman's attempt to impose some sort of order on the chaos of living in Belfast during The Troubles. Just as she destroys Cassie's dream of escape by stealing her £200, Deirdre symbolically destroys Nora's dream by slashing the 'fifteen yards of peach polyester' and 'trampling it till she's breathless'.

Evidence of wider knowledge of the text.

Even this setback does not get Nora down for long. As the plot moves towards the climactic final scenes of the drama, Nora says defiantly, 'Well I'm going up the town tomorrow. I'm just going to go up the town and buy a piece of what I want. I'll get credit and I'll have my loose covers.'

Reference to an appropriate dramatic technique.

The audience is left with an image of a woman who has been through a lot and yet still refuses to give in. The skillful characterisation of Nora presents us with a very human character with all the usual human failings and yet someone who has an inner strength and resolve. As Nora tells us herself:

A reference back to the question itself – always refer back to the question at the end of your essay.

'I've poems in my head as good as anyone.'

Practice essay questions

You can use the following questions to practise your critical essay writing skills.

Remember that the types of questions you get asked tend to fall into groups. Prepare yourself to write about theme, character, setting, structure, etc.

Drama

- Choose a play in which one character mistrusts another character.

  Explain the nature of this mistrust and explain how it affects the outcome of the play.

- Choose a play that contains a strong female character.

  Briefly describe the character's role in the play and go on to explain how her strength is revealed to the audience.

- Choose a play that explores the theme of survival.

  With reference to appropriate dramatic techniques, show how this theme is presented to the audience.

- Choose a play that relies on more than just dialogue to achieve dramatic effects.

  Explain how the playwright makes use of these techniques to achieve these effects.

- Choose a play that explores the relationship between parents and their children.

  By making reference to specific dramatic techniques, show how the dramatist presents this theme to the audience.

- Choose a play in which the main character is isolated from those around him or her.

  Briefly describe the nature of the isolation and go on to show how this affects the drama as a whole.

- Choose a play in which there is a mixture of sadness and comedy.

  Briefly describe how these elements are presented in the play and go on to show how they add to the overall effectiveness of the drama.

- Choose a play in which a key scene reveals something significant about the main character.

  Briefly describe what happens and go on to show the significance of the scene to the play as a whole.

- Choose a play that you think ends in a particularly satisfying way.

  Describe what happens and go on to explain why you found the ending particularly satisfying.

- Choose a play that makes use of unconventional staging techniques.

  Show how the use of these techniques enables the dramatist to convey important themes to the audience.

- Choose a play which, despite being set in a specific time and place, manages to explore issues that are important to us all.

  Briefly describe the setting and go on to discuss the dramatist's exploration of these issues.

Prose

- Choose a novel **or** a short story in which the author creates a character for whom you develop a feeling of admiration.

  With reference to appropriate techniques, show how the author has created this character and why you admire him/her.

- Choose a novel **or** a short story in which the use of setting adds to the overall effectiveness of the text.

  Briefly describe the setting(s) and explain how this feature adds to the effectiveness of the text.

- Choose a novel that has a particularly satisfying ending.

  Briefly describe the ending and go on to explain how the writer's use of particular techniques makes it a satisfying one for the reader.

- Choose a novel **or** a short story which explores an important theme (love, death, isolation, loss, change …).

  With reference to appropriate techniques, explain how the writer reveals this theme to the reader.

- Choose a novel or short story that is set in Scotland.
  Briefly describe the setting and go on to explain why the particular setting is important to the text as a whole.
- Choose a novel or short story in which there is a character with whom you closely identify.
  By making reference to specific literary techniques, show how the author has succeeded in making you identify with this character.
- Choose a novel or short story that makes effective use of structure.
  Show how the writer's use of structure adds to the overall effectiveness of the text.
- Choose a novel or short story with an unconventional hero.
  Briefly describe the unconventional aspects of this character and go on to show how they contribute to the central concerns of the text.
- Choose a novel or short story that explores the theme of relationships.
  By making reference to specific literary techniques, show how the writer presents this theme to the reader.
- Choose a novel or short story that seemed simple when you first read it but more complex when you read it a second time.
  By referring to specific elements of the text, show how the writer has created this complexity.
- Choose a non-fiction text which seems to teach the reader an important lesson about life.
  Briefly describe the 'lesson' and explain how the author's use of particular techniques adds to the effectiveness of his or her writing.
- Choose a non-fiction text that reveals something about the writer.
  By referring to specific techniques, show how the text does this.

Poetry

- Choose a poem in which the form and structure chosen by the poet is particularly suited to the subject matter of the poem.
  Show how the poet has made use of form and structure to create a successful poem.
- Choose a poem that celebrates a positive aspect of life.
  Show how the poet's use of a range of poetic techniques helps to show this to the reader.
- Choose a poem that makes use of colloquial or informal language.
  Briefly say what the poem is about and go on to show how the poet's use of colloquial or informal language adds to the impact of the poem.

- Choose a poem that explores a serious theme.

  With reference to appropriate poetic techniques, show how this theme is explored in the poem.

- Choose two poems by the same poet that explore a similar theme.

  Show how the poet explores the theme in each poem and go on to discuss which poem you prefer and why.

- Choose a poem in which the form and structure seem particularly suited to the subject matter.

  Briefly say what the poem is about and go on to show how the form and structure of the poem particularly suit the subject matter.

- Choose a poem in which the poet adopts a persona.

  Show how the use of a persona adds to the overall effectiveness of the text.

- Choose a poem written long ago.

  Show how, despite being written long ago, the text still has something to say to the reader of today.

- Choose a poem that deals with a powerful emotion such as love, hate, fear or anger.

  By referring to specific poetic techniques, show how the poet conveys the emotion to the reader.

- Choose a poem in which the use of sound is particularly important.

  Briefly say what the poem is about and go on to show how the poet's use of sound is particularly important to the text as a whole.

- Choose a poem which seems especially suited to a teenage reader.

  Briefly say what the poem is about and go on to explain how the poet has constructed something that appeals to this audience.

Film and TV drama

- Choose a film **or** TV drama in which there is a main character for whom you feel dislike.

  Show how media techniques are used to portray the character in such a way that we feel dislike.

- Choose an opening scene or sequence from a film **or** TV drama that you consider to be particularly effective.

  Briefly describe what happens in the scene or sequence and go on to explain how the use of particular media techniques contribute to the effectiveness.

- Choose a film **or** TV drama that explores an issue relevant to young people today in an interesting way.

  Briefly describe the issue and then show how media techniques are used to explore it in an interesting way.

- Choose a film or TV drama that captures your interest right from the start.

  By referring to specific techniques, show how the director captures your attention in this way.

Language

- Consider the different forms of language you use depending on the situation you are in.

  By giving examples of distinctive vocabulary **or** grammatical constructions, show how your language changes in these different situations.

- Consider the language in advertisements for Scottish products.

  By discussing the language of one such advertisement, identify the key features that vary from other types of advertising and explain why these features could appeal to the target audience.

What you have to do

As well as sitting the question paper, you must send a portfolio of your best writing to the SQA for assessment.

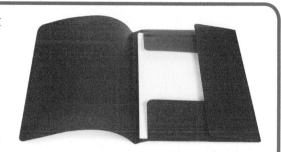

You must submit two pieces of writing, each from a different genre. Each piece will be marked out of 15 and the total score of 30 for the portfolio will be added to your marks from the question paper to decide your final grade of A, B, C, etc.

The writing pieces are your responsibility but they will be written under supervision and control. This means that you might submit a plan and a first draft to your teacher who will then make suggestions to help you improve your work. You would then take the piece away again and complete a final draft. SQA regulations for this qualification state that 'No assessed piece may be redrafted more than twice' (SQA 2012).

The work must be your own. You cannot copy content from elsewhere or have a teacher, tutor or parent write any of it for you. There are severe penalties for plagiarism. You must list any sources you have consulted in your writing (for example give the URL address for websites).

- Each piece should be no more than 1,000 words long.
- Each piece should be typed and printed on A4 paper.

EXAM TIP

Make things easy for your marker and always use a simple font for the writing you send to SQA.
- Times New Roman, Ariel, and Calibri are all suitable fonts.
- 12 point is an effective font size to use.
- Use black ink for all text.

What the writing portfolio must contain

As stated above, your writing portfolio must contain **two** pieces of writing: a **creative** piece and a **discursive** piece.

Group A – creative	Group B – discursive
A personal/reflective essay.	A piece of transactional writing.
A piece of prose fiction (e.g. a short story, an episode from a novel).	A persuasive essay.
A poem or set of thematically linked poems.	An argumentative essay.
A dramatic script (e.g. a scene, monologue, sketch).	A report for a specified purpose.

You should already be familiar with most of these genres from your work in your previous Curriculum for Excellence English courses. As long as you choose one piece from Group A and one from Group B, your writing portfolio will be acceptable to the SQA. For example:

- A short story and a persuasive piece on why all pupils should use smartphones in class.
- A poem and a report on the time allocated to PE in Scottish schools.
- A single-scene drama script and an argumentative essay that explores the topic of social media.
- A reflective essay on why snowboarding is important to you and a transactional piece giving information on the discipline system used in your school.

Let's look at how your writing pieces will be marked. Your marker will allocate each piece to a category and then decide on a final mark within that category. The table below shows what the features of a **very good** piece of writing are (Category 1) and the features of a piece of writing that is **just good enough** to pass (Category 3).

EXAM TIP

This is the one element of your assessment that is entirely under your control. As it is worth 30% of your overall mark, it makes sense to put as much effort into this as you can. **Don't** allow yourself to hand in work that is not the best you can possibly do. **Don't** leave everything to the last minute. Ask advice from your teacher/tutor as early as possible.

Writing which is broadly creative

Range of marks	15–13	9–7
Content	Attention to purpose and audience is consistent. As appropriate to genre: • The piece displays very good creativity • Feeling/reaction/experiences are expressed/explored with a very good degree of self-awareness/involvement/insight sensitivity	Attention to purpose and audience is reasonably well sustained. As appropriate to genre: • The piece shows some creativity • Feeling/reactions/experiences are explored with a sense of involvement
Style	• The features of the chosen genre are deployed effectively • Word choice is varied and often used to create particular effects • The structure of the piece enhances the purpose/meaning	• The features of the chosen genre are deployed with a degree of success • Word choice is effective in the main • The structure of the piece is appropriate to purpose/meaning

Writing which is broadly discursive

Range of marks	15–13	9–7
Content	• Attention to purpose and audience is consistent • Information shows evidence of careful research, is presented to maximise impact and is sequenced to highlight key points • Ideas/techniques deployed to inform/argue/discuss/persuade have a very good degree of objectivity/depth/insight, persuasive force and are used to convey a clear line of thought/appropriate stance/point of view	• Attention to purpose and audience is reasonably well sustained • Information shows evidence of some research and is presented in a clear sequence • Ideas/techniques deployed to inform/argue/discuss/persuade convey a line of thought/stance/point of view
Style	• The features of the chosen genre are deployed effectively • Word choice is varied and often used to create particular effects • The structure of the piece enhances the purpose/meaning	• The features of the chosen genre are deployed, mostly successfully • Word choice is apposite and used at times to create and effect • The structure of the piece supports the purpose/meaning

Satisfactory technical accuracy is a requirement for a mark of 8 or above. Writing may contain errors, but these will not be significant. Paragraphing, sentence construction, spelling and punctuation should be sufficiently accurate so that meaning is clear at the first reading.

SQA 2011

Here's a reminder of the writing process.

1. **Your proposal** – your ideas for the piece of writing.

2. **An outline plan** – which shows the structure of your writing.

3. **A first draft** – your teacher will give you feedback on this.

4. **A second draft** – to be submitted to the SQA.

At all stages of the process you should be thinking about **T.A.P.**

- The **type** of writing you are producing (use genre markers effectively).
- The **audience** it is aimed at (don't forget that ultimately the audience is your examiner).
- The **purpose** of the piece (to entertain, to persuade, to shock, etc.).

How to produce an effective piece of writing

Now let's look at how you might produce two pieces of writing for the folio: a reflective essay (creative) and an argumentative essay (discursive).

Reflective writing

In reflective writing, it's vital to show that you are reflecting on the experience and not just describing a personal experience. Remember to include your thoughts and feelings. If possible, try to avoid subjects that examiners will have seen many times before, e.g. the death of a grandparent; moving from primary to secondary school, etc. Ask your teacher/tutor for advice if you are in any doubt.

Riding goofy – what snowboarding means to me

Let's consider a reflective essay on a hobby or sport you enjoy. Here is a possible structure with some starter sentences for each paragraph that you could take and adapt for a wide variety of reflective pieces:

Paragraph 1 – Say what it is you like about the activity – think about this (reflect) as you describe getting your gear ready for a day on the slopes. Describe what your first run feels like and reflect on your feelings of excitement. Describe what it feels like to complete a challenging descent or pull off a new trick. Start like this:

It's still dark as I get into the car and head for the Lecht. Most people are still in bed but getting up isn't difficult for me when I'm about to spend the day doing what I love best – snowboarding with my friends.

Paragraph 2 – Now shift the focus from your own experience to consider snowboarding in a wider context. You might begin this paragraph with:

Other people might wonder what the point of my sport is. They don't understand that what they get at a football match or by playing on their Xbox or from buying that pair of heels, I get from being on my board.

Paragraph 3 – Consider what other people think of you doing this activity. You might begin:

To be honest, I know my mum is terrified every time she watches me trying out a new trick.

Paragraph 4 – Compare your experiences to those of others.

Shaun Whyte, the best snowboarder on the planet, says 'It's about pushing yourself to try new things and do the unexpected. Finally, and most importantly, it's about being creative.' I know exactly what he means.

Paragraph 5 – Return to a description of the activity.

I take the chairlift to the top of the mountain. I feel anticipation, excitement and yes, even a little fear.

Paragraph 6 – Describe how the activity has changed your life.

Confidence. Friendship. Challenge. These are the things that snowboarding has given me.

Argumentative writing

In this kind of writing you have to consider at least **two** sides of an argument on a particular topic. The most straightforward structure is first to consider the **pros** (the arguments for), and then to consider the **cons** (the arguments against), before finally coming to a conclusion. This simple structure has the great advantage of keeping your line of thought clear for the reader.

Again, try to choose a topic that means something to you – your examiner will have read all the essays he or she could ever wish to on animal testing, overpaid footballers, the death penalty, etc. Ask your teacher/tutor for advice.

EXAM TIP

Always choose a topic for your discursive writing that means something to you – you will almost always produce a better piece of writing if you do.

Smartphones in classrooms

Let's consider an argumentative essay on the use of smartphones in the classroom. Here is a possible structure; some appropriate techniques to use and starter sentences for each paragraph. Again, you could easily adapt this approach to other topics.

Paragraph 1 – Introduce the topic. Notice the use of questions to involve the reader.

The use of smartphones in classrooms has become a contentious issue in schools in recent months. Most pupils carry one of these miniature computers and you can see them being used on the way to school, on the way home from school and in school social areas. Should we now allow these devices to be used in classrooms? Or are there too many dangers associated with them?

Paragraph 2 – Make your first point. An argument *for*.

One argument in favour of using smartphones in the classroom is that pupils can use them to make a note of any homework given out. This means that we can do away with bulky paper planners and homework diaries.

Paragraph 3 – Make your second point. Always try to link the sections or paragraphs in your writing effectively.

As well as this, smartphones can be used as calculators in maths and science.

Paragraph 4 – Now make your next point. Notice the use of evidence here.

In addition to these uses, the best thing about a smartphone is that it lets you access the internet. You can research information for your subjects online or download materials from your school website. You no longer have to go to a school computer suite to do this – you can do all these things in class. Last year, a study in Manchester showed that pupils improved their test scores by 15% if they were allowed access to smartphones in class.

Paragraph 5 – Now put forward the final argument *for*.

Furthermore, as school is supposed to prepare pupils for the world of work where smartphones are in use all the time, it seems only right that pupils learn to work with these devices in school.

Paragraph 6 – Now discuss the *cons* – the arguments *against*.

Despite all these positives, there are also dangers in allowing pupils to use smartphones in class. The first one to consider is that films of teachers and pupils could be posted on the internet without their knowledge.

Paragraph 7 – Make your next point.

Secondly, there is the argument that pupils might be distracted by emails and messages received during a lesson.

Paragraph 8 – Consider your final *con* or argument *against*.

Finally, what do schools do for pupils who do not have a smartphone?

Paragraph 9 – Your conclusion.

It is clear that there are some convincing arguments against having smartphones in the classroom. It is also clear, however, that schools need to keep up with new technology and that the advantages of using smartphones in class outweigh the disadvantages.

Don't forget to acknowledge any sources (print, digital, TV or film) you have consulted. You can simply list these at the end of your writing, for example:

http://news.bbc.co.uk/1/hi/school_report/9433970.stm

http://www.bbc.co.uk/news/education-21476385

'Judo: Renicks eager to take sister act to Glasgow', *The Herald*, Friday 15 March 2013

Ideas for creative writing

Personal reflective

- Why snowboarding is important to me.
- What my team means to me.
- Sibling rivalry.
- The animals in my life.
- A narrow escape – and what it taught me.
- A keepsake that means a lot to me.
- What I've gained from performing in front of others.
- Living in Scotland today.
- My family.
- Friends.
- The passing of time.
- Challenges I have faced.
- The important things in life are …
- Solitude.

Prose fiction

Titles
- Trapped!
- The waiting game
- Star
- An appointment with death
- The Magic Box
- Speed
- The Network
- Playing with fire

Starters
- Kirsty walked into the office. Silence. She hadn't expected this …
- It is a truth universally acknowledged that a Scotsman in possession of a carry out must be in want of a party.
- 50 clicks still to go and only enough fuel for 20. Commander Grant looked round at his rag tag army …
- I rang the bell. No response. I rang it again. Still nothing. I rang it for a third time. From somewhere deep inside that old house I heard someone *or something* begin to move.
- Fiona looked at the faces around the table. 'I'm not sure I even know these people anymore,' she thought to herself.

Poetry

Anything is a potential subject for a poem. Why not choose a particular verse form to express your ideas? Perhaps a sonnet or a villanelle?

A dramatic script

- Two friends fall out on their way home from school.
- A game of cards (who might the players be?).
- A young person visiting an elderly relative in a care home.
- Three people waiting to be interviewed for a job.
- A court room scene.
- Two people on a first date.
- An unexpected guest interrupts a family celebration.
- A psychiatrist and a patient.
- A son or daughter having to apologise to their parents for some misdemeanour.
- A corner shop and its eccentric owner.
- A dramatic monologue from the point of view of a small child.
- Three people stuck in a lift.

Discursive writing

- A transactional essay that gives information on the discipline system used in your school.
- An argumentative essay that explores the topic of social media.
- A persuasive essay on why all pupils should use smartphones in class.
- A report on the time allocated to PE in Scottish schools.
- A persuasive essay on what needs to be done to improve Scottish football.
- An argumentative essay on 'is Scotland a truly multicultural society?'
- A persuasive essay on why you shouldn't go to university.
- An argumentative essay on single-sex schools.
- A report on the different languages used in Scotland today.
- An argumentative piece on Scottish independence.
- A persuasive essay on the benefits of renewable energy.
- An argumentative essay on the influence of religion on our lives.

More study and revision advice

You'll probably spend 4.5–5 hours in your English class each week for the National 5 course. If you are going to maximise your chances of success you need to put in a significant amount of study time over and above what you do in school.

Here are some reminders about what you should be doing throughout your course:

- If you don't understand anything in class, ask your teacher at the end of the period or ask if you can speak to them at a later date – never forget that your teacher is the best resource you have.

- Make use of any study periods or dedicated revision classes offered at school.

- Set aside some time each night (on at least Monday–Thursday) to review what you learned that day in English class.

- Write down quotations from your texts onto Post-it notes and display them where you will see them regularly.

- Give yourself small tests on quotations, names of characters, techniques – anything you feel you need to remember for the exam.

- Keep a writer's notebook to jot down ideas for the pieces in your portfolio.

- Don't just make written notes – draw pictures, create diagrams or anything else that suits your learning style.
- Break down your revision into manageable sections.
- Buy cheap copies of your texts and annotate and highlight relevant content.
- Look on the internet for other resources – but ask your teacher to check if they're suitable.
- Consult the following websites:
    - http://www.sqa.org.uk/sqa/45674.html. This is the SQA's National 5 site.
    - https://secure.glowscotland.org.uk/login/login.htm. GLOW – log in with the username and password provided by your school.
    - http://www.bbc.co.uk/bitesize/higher/english/cone_gatherers/. BBC Cone Gatherers site, which is useful for revising the novel.
    - https://bubbl.us/. An easy-to-use mind-map/revision tool.
    - https://cramberry.net/. Create your own revision flashcards online.
    - http://www.sparknotes.com/. Useful for revision of popular non-Scottish texts.
    - http://www.shmoop.com/. Useful for revision of popular non-Scottish texts.

Answers

Reading skills: how to infer things, pages 10–11

1.	Where is this passage set?
	Inference: In a city
	Clues:
	• Reference to 'bombsites'.
	• In the 1960s many cities still had areas left derelict after German bombing raids.
2.	Who do you think 'we' are?
	Inference: The narrator and his friends/his gang
	Clues:
	• The activities they get up to.
	• The list of names.
3.	What is a Swan Vesta?
	Inference: A brand of match.
	Clues:
	• 'Playful match' in the previous sentence.
	• Reference to 'fire' in the second paragraph.
4.	Why is Peter referred to as Kingy?
	Inference: His surname is 'King'
	Clues:
	• He's one of the gang.
	• We often add –y to a name to form a nickname.
5.	What is a Ford Popular?
	Inference: An old make (and model) of car.
	Clues: Reference to 'banger' and 'rusted old vehicle'.
6.	From what sort of text is this passage taken?
	Inference: The correct answer is 'autobiography' but you could also legitimately say novel, because many novels are written in the first person.
	Clues:
	• First person narration.
	• Memorable event (with an especially memorable opening line).
	• Contrast with 'kids these days'.
	• Cliffhanger ending.

Reading skills: how to summarise texts, pages 12–13

Your seven bullet points might look something like these:
- Three young Scots dressed up in one-piece suits from Japan for a night out in Canada.
- Lots of people were interested in the suits.
- The decided to make their own version of the suits to make some money.
- Their company has grown very quickly.
- The morphsuits have become very popular worldwide.
- The morphsuits are used in a wide variety of ways.
- The company is making lots of money.

Reading skills: identifying and analysing, page 15

You should have identified the following techniques.
- Alliteration –'**g**rey day … **g**reat prison'; '**s**ix-year **s**entence'.
- Metaphor – 'great prison' to describe his school.
- Simile – 'slipping away like a ship being launched into the sea'.
- Onomatopoeia 'buzz of classroom voices'.
- Personification – 'the dark figure of mathematics wouldn't let him escape, and soon chased after him'.

Quick test, page 17

1. Identify the language features used in the following sentences.
    (a) simile
    (b) colon to introduce a list; semi-colons to separate items in the list
    (c) onomatopoeia
    (d) parenthesis (a description of the building)
    (e) metaphor, alliteration, onomatopoeia
    (f) alliteration, inversion
    (g) personification, alliteration
    (h) simile
    (i) climax
    (j) rhetorical questions
    (k) minor sentence
    (l) onomatopoeia
    (m) minor sentence
    (n) alliteration
    (o) colon to introduce a list, semi-colons to separate items in the list
2. Have a look at the following texts and see how many language features you can spot. You should also comment on the *effect* created by the writer.
    (a) alliteration – 'burning brightly' helps to draw the reader's eye to these words; repetition – 'no way … No way' emphasises the difficulty of his situation; repeated structure building to a climax – 'Not today. Not tomorrow. Not ever.' suggests the utter hopelessness of his situation.
    (b) repetition – 'closer and closer'; 'louder and louder' as the writer builds to a climax ('his opportunity was here at last'); repetition – 'Would you … would you …' suggests his nervousness; anticlimax – 'would you pass me the salt, please?' when the reader is expecting him to ask the girl out.
    (c) rhetorical questions – invite the reader to agree with the writer's anti-uniform stance.
    (d) inversion – 'Excitedly' placed at the start of the sentence to highlight the narrator's state of mind; parenthesis – '(a gleaming silver BMW)', which adds information about the car's make and appearance; colon – to introduce the list of what the narrator loved about the car; semi-colon – to separate items in the list; onomatopoeia – 'roar' to suggest the sound and power of the engine.

Practice unit assessment: analysis and
evaluation – reading, pages 20–21

National 5 – Understand, analyse and evaluate *detailed* written texts

Identify and explain the purpose and audience as appropriate to genre.	• Can deduce the purpose and audience, giving appropriate textual justification.	For q 1. you should identify a possible audience for the poem and then justify your answer with evidence from the text. In this case you *could* say 'someone interested in poetry'! You might say 'teachers' or 'students' and quote evidence that suggests the learning/teaching situation alluded to in the poem. *Any* reasonable answer would be fine as long as it is supported with evidence from the text.
	• Can identify the generic conventions of fiction and non-fiction texts.	For q 6. you might say: • to show that poetry is not meant to be analysed in this way • how we teach and learn poetry is wrong • to make us question how we teach poetry • to entertain • or any other reasonable answer.
Identify the main idea and supporting details.	• Can clearly identify the most relevant points.	For q 2. you might say 'a teacher' or 'a lecturer' or even just the poet himself. For q 3. you might say '*his* students/pupils'.
	• Can infer from the passage, drawing on appropriate evidence.	For q 4. (a) you might say 'he wants his pupils to respond imaginatively to (or just enjoy) a poem'. For q 4. (b) you might say 'he doesn't succeed' and refer to either of the images in the last two stanzas.
Apply knowledge and understanding of language to explain meaning and effect, using appropriate critical terminology.	• Can identify and analyse various features of a writer's use of language and its effect.	For q 5. (a) and (b) you are free to choose any three examples. For example, you might quote any appropriate examples of imagery or word choice in stanzas 1–5. You might then refer to the effect of these techniques and what they suggest a poem is: something colourful or alive; something in which sound is important; something that involves exploration or discovery; something which is an active experience; something enjoyable.
	• Can use appropriate textual reference or quotation.	You might also refer to the imagery or word choice in the final two stanzas and offer suitable analysis/comments.

Understanding, analysis and evaluation questions, pages 34–37

		Marks
1.	Read the first paragraph. **In your own words**, describe the change that takes place in the conversation between the writer and the Renicks sisters. To answer this you need to *locate* the part of the passage that contains the answer and then *translate* it into your own words. You would get 1 mark for describing 'unrelenting' e.g. *non-stop* or describing 'candid', e.g. *truthful*, and 1 mark for describing 'curtailed', e.g. *is brought to a stop*.	2
2.	Look at lines 10–15. **In your own words**, explain why Louise 'instinctively assumes authority' over her younger sister. • Locate the answer and translate it into your own words. • A 'consequence of her initial dominance in their contests', e.g. usually beat her sister (1 mark) when they first started to compete against each other (1 mark). • She has to do the driving/Kimberley has not yet passed her driving test (1 mark).	3
3.	Look at lines 26–61. **In your own words**, explain the difficulties *Kimberley* has had to overcome in her judo career. Another locate and translate exercise for you. This time the information is spread out more widely in the passage. Possible answers, with any four for 1 mark each: • issues with her weight • didn't always eat the right things • found it difficult to cope with her feelings when she fought her sister • dealing with her mother's illness • missing out on the London Olympics.	4
4.	Explain how the writer's use of sentence structure helps to clarify the information conveyed to the reader in lines 66–74. You should refer to two examples in your answer. Possible answers: • Parenthesis is used in lines 66–67 (just a week …) (1) to show the tight time scale (1 mark). • A colon in line 69 (1) introduces the reasons why the sisters can't 'afford to slack' (1 mark). • A semi-colon is used to separate the reasons (1 mark). • Repetition/climax in line 74 'even more … more … more …' (1 mark) is used to suggest the extent of the task facing the girls in attempting to qualify (1 mark).	4

5.	Look at lines 78–81. **In your words**, explain what Louise tells the writer about in this paragraph. Example answers: • The regular drug testing she undergoes (1 mark). • The care she takes to avoid drinks that might have been tampered with ('spiked') (1 mark). • The fact she seems wary of everyone/the length of time it's taken her to trust her partner to get her a drink (1 mark).	**3**
6.	Look at lines 82–88. In your own words, explain the different ways the sisters respond when challenged by 'guys with a drink in them'. You would be awarded 2 marks for a full explanation of each sister's response and 1 mark for a more basic explanation. Kimberley: • manages to avoid the confrontation because of her size ('uses her diminutive figure to deny her status'). Louise: • always defends her sister ('ever the protector') • not as cautious ('less circumspect') • gets very angry ('the rage comes') • reacts physically ('throw people over tables …').	**4**
7.	What do you think the use of Scots words adds to this article? You should refer to specific examples in your answer. Any two of the following answers, supported by the appropriate quotation: • Allows the writer to reproduce how the girls actually speak ('Aye …'). • Suggests the low opinion the sisters' (and the writer) have of 'guys with a drink in them' ('chancers and bams'). • Adds humour ('neddy boys'). • Suggests 'typically Scottish' willingness to stand up for yourself ('aye, okay then, I dare ye').	**4**

8.	Choose one of the following images: • 'exchange steely looks' (line 4) • 'bristles ever so slightly' (line 7) • 'look at you as a trophy' (line 85) Explain what your chosen image means and analyse its effect. You would be awarded 3 marks for a full analysis of the image; 2 marks for a clear analysis and 1 mark for a weak analysis. You must always state what the comparison is. • 'Steely looks' suggests something hard and unyielding. • 'The older sister bristles' suggests she reacts like an animal does when threatened, i.e. the hairs on the back of a dog's neck go up. • 'A trophy' suggests something to be won/something to show off as a symbol of success. Example answers: • The way the girls look at each other is compared to a hard metal. This shows their determination and how strong minded they are. • Louise's reaction is compared to an animal feeling threatened. This suggests that she doesn't agree with or doesn't like the way her sister describes her. • Some (men) regard the girls as something to be won, just as a trophy is a prize gained for achieving something.	3
9.	Identify the writer's attitude to the Renicks sisters in this article and give two pieces of evidence to support your answer. • Correctly identifying the writer's attitude – admiration/respect (1 mark). • Giving two pieces of evidence (there are many examples in this passage) (2 marks).	3
	Total	**20**

Bold Girls, by Rona Munro, pages 40–43

1.	In what ways are Marie's actions in the stage direction in line 2 typical of this character? They show that she is hospitable or caring or 'domestic' (1 mark).	1
2.	'Though it seems to me there's not a place in the world that is different' (lines 13–14). What does this suggest about Nora's view of life? It suggests she has a very cynical outlook (1 mark) or that it doesn't matter what you do you can't escape from the problems in your life (1 mark).	1

3.	What is the effect of the stage direction in line 21 'no one says anything else for a second'? It suggests Nora is shocked or surprised by the news (1 mark). It increases the dramatic tension (1 mark).	2
4.	Comment on the word choice and imagery of Nora's line 'tear them out by the roots and drag them along after you' (lines 35–36). 'Tear' and 'drag' suggest this would be a violent act (1 mark, 'drag' also suggests they would be unwilling to go (1 mark). 'out by the roots' suggests the children are being removed from the place they are growing up in/belong to/are being nurtured in (like a plant) (1 mark).	2
5.	What sort of look do you think Marie gives Cassie in line 39? • Disbelief – she's a mother herself and can't believe Cassie would actually do something like this. • Reproach – she doesn't think it is something Cassie should do. • Either answer – or similar – plus suitable comment for 1 mark.	1
6.	Why might it be considered ironic that Cassie chose to hide the money behind the picture of Michael? She had also hidden – from Marie – (1 mark) her affair with Michael (1 mark).	2
7.	What do lines 109–118 suggest about Nora? Support your answer with evidence from the text. • She seems determined 'I'm just going to go up the town and buy a piece of what I want.' • She's not well-off and finds money difficult to come by – like all the women in the play 'I'll give them a false address and I'll get credit.' • She's become emotionally 'harder' because of what's happened to her – 'had to grow it that way.' • 1 mark for each point.	3
8.	This extract illustrates the theme of broken dreams in the play. Choose another theme that is explored in the play and briefly describe how Rona Munro presents it to the audience. You might describe the dramatic treatment of one of the following: • relationships • truth and deception • friendship and solidarity • survival • domestic abuse • 1 mark for each valid point/reference/comment made.	8
	Total	**20**

'The Telegram', by Iain Crichton Smith, pages 44–47

1.	What does the imagery used to describe the two women in paragraph 1 (lines 3–5) suggest about their appearance and personalities?	2
	• 'A fat domestic bird', 'fat' obviously suggests the large size of this woman.	
	• 'Domestic' perhaps suggests someone who is docile and settled in her life.	
	• The image perhaps also contains the idea of the woman being a contented housewife	
	• 'More aquiline, more gaunt' suggests the other woman is more slender with perhaps a very haughty or proud appearance ('aquiline' means 'like an eagle'; if your nose is 'aquiline' it's hooked or curved like a bird of prey's beak).	
	• 'Like a buzzard' is another way the writer suggests that she perhaps looks rather fierce.	
	• 1 mark for each valid point you make but you must comment on the descriptions of both women for maximum marks.	
2.	Identify the technique the writer uses to describe the war in paragraph 3 (lines 18–19) and comment on its effectiveness.	3
	Metaphor (1 mark). It's an effective image because 'strange' suggests the villagers couldn't understand it (1 mark) and 'plague' suggests something that kills many people (1 mark).	
3.	Which word, used later in the passage, continues the idea contained in 'plague'?	1
	'Feverishly' (1 mark).	
4.	'… the village which was still, as it had always been, a superstitious place.' (paragraph 2)	
	How does the women's behaviour later in this extract illustrate the superstitious nature of the villagers?	1
	You should make reference to paragraph 10: '… as if by speaking continually and watching his every move they would be able to keep themselves from whatever plague he was bringing.' (1 mark).	
5.	What is surprising about the description of the thin woman as 'an incomer'?	2
	She has lived there for thirty years (1 mark) so it is strange she is still regarded as an outsider (1 mark).	

6.	What does this description of the thin woman suggest about the village where the story is set? • It's a very close-knit community. • That not much changes in the village. • Suspicious of 'outsiders'. • Inward looking. • Any two. • 1 mark for each valid point made.	2
7.	What can you infer about the thin woman's lifestyle from the information in this extract? • It is not lavish in any way. • She's on her own – her husband is dead. • Her pension is not much to live on. • She has given up a lot to support her son's studies. • Any one for 1 mark.	1
8.	Show how the use of setting in this short story is similar or different to another short story by Iain Crichton Smith you have studied. • Reference to use of setting in 'The Telegram' (2 marks) plus related comment (2 marks). • Reference to use of setting in another story by Iain Crichton Smith (2 marks) plus related comment (up to 2 marks).	8
	Total	**20**

'All that Glisters', by Anne Donovan pages, 48–49

1.	Using your own words, describe the narrator's reaction to being asked 'tae make Christmas cards wi coloured cardboard and felties'? • She thinks the task is rather childish (description of 'a bit much when we're in second year') (1). • She likes it/thinks it's an easy option (description of 'better than daein real work') (1).	2
2. (a)	What is the difference between the language used by the supply teacher and the language used by Clare? • The narrator, Clare, tells us the story in Scots (1). • The supply teacher speaks in standard English (1).	1

Answers

2. (b)	Why do you think Anne Donovan has chosen to show this difference? • To add realism to the story. • To suggest the setting of the story. • To suggest education is delivered in English not Scots. • To make Clare a believable character. • To show the reader Clare's thoughts and feelings more clearly. • To show a contrast between Clare and her teacher. • Any two of the above, (1) mark each.	**2**	
3.	Claire describes the glitter pens ('rid, green, gold and silver'). Why is the reference to colour an important feature of this extract? • Clare thinks they bring things 'tae life'. • Reference to 'the difference between a Christmas tree skinklin wi fairy lights an wan lyin deid an daurk in a corner.' • The colourful card cheers up Clare's father. • Contrasts with the description of Clare's father as 'a ghost'. • Any two of the above, (1) mark each.	**2**	
4.	What does the reader learn about Clare's father in lines 28–44? Use your own words in your answer. • He's seriously ill. • He's had a cough for a long time. • He has been unable to work for a long time. • His condition has worsened over the last three months. • He used to work demolishing buildings. • Asbestos in the dust has caused his illness. • Reference to at least two of the above (1 mark). • Reference to at least four of the above (2 marks).	**2**	
5. (a)	Why might Clare's father's statement 'They cried it the funeral dress of kings' (lines 51–52) be considered ironic • It is ironic given that Clare's father – an ordinary working man (1) is dying from being covered in asbestos (1 mark).	**2**	
5. (b)	Identify and comment on another example of irony from the extract. • 'He used tae kid on he wis a ghost' • 'Comes fae a Greek word that means indestructible' • 'Ma daddy wis dead chuffed' • Reference to any one of the above accompanied by an appropriate comment, 1 mark each.	**1**	
6.	Show how the language and ideas of this short story are similar or different to another short story by Anne Donovan you have read. • Reference to an idea/use of language from this story (1 mark) plus related comment (up to 2 marks). • Reference to an idea/use of language from another story by Donovan (2 marks) plus related comment (up to 2 marks).	**8**	

'Originally', by Carol Ann Duffy, pages 50–51

1.	How does the poet's language convey contrasting moods in the first stanza?	3
	• The mother is 'singing', which suggests a happy/optimistic mood (1 mark).	
	And any two of:	
	• 'Cried' and 'bawling' suggests the brothers' unhappiness (1 mark).	
	• 'Blind toy' could be seen as an unpleasant image: something maimed or incomplete (or it might just reflect the age of the toy!); suggests mood of unease (1 mark).	
	• 'Holding its paw' suggests the speaker's feeling of unease and her desire to be comforted (1 mark).	
	• 'Fell through the fields' suggests the speed of the journey and so perhaps creates a sense of helplessness (1 mark).	
2.	'All childhood is an emigration.' (line 9). What do you think the poet means by this?	2
	• You would get 2 marks for a full answer, such as: *This metaphor suggests that growing up involves leaving things behind and going on to a new/strange place.*	
	• You would get 1 mark for a more basic point, for example: *It suggests childhood involves moving from one stage of life to another.*	
3.	'My parents' anxiety stirred like a loose tooth in my head.' (lines 15–16). Why is this an effective and appropriate simile to use in this context?	2
	• It effectively suggests that the speaker realises the concern felt by the parents about moving their children to a new life in a new country and that she keeps thinking about it (just like your tongue keeps going to a loose tooth in your mouth) (1 mark).	
	• The comparison is appropriate given the presumed age of the speaker at this point in the poem (young enough to be losing her baby teeth) (1 mark).	
4.	'… feel only a skelf of shame.' (lines 18–19). Why is this an effective and appropriate metaphor to use in this context?	2
	• It is effective because by comparing her shame to a small splinter it shows how much her sense of shame has diminished/how much she is now used to her new life (1 mark).	
	• It is appropriate because it is a Scots word and the poem is concerned with the speaker's loss of 'culture, speech' (1 mark).	

5.	'I remember my tongue/shedding its skin like a snake' (lines 19–20). Why is this an effective and appropriate image to use in this context?	2
	You might mention any two of the following:	
	• A snake is often a symbol of evil or treachery (the speaker perhaps feels she is betraying her past) (1 mark).	
	• Suggests the change in her language is a natural (inevitable) thing (1 mark).	
	• It's a positive image of change and renewal (1 mark).	
	• Use of alliteration/sibilance ('skin … snake') is appropriate given the snake image (1 mark).	
6.	Why does the speaker 'hesitate' in the final line of the poem?	1
	She finds it difficult to say where her origins lie/she feels she has lost her original identity (1 mark).	
7.	Is the use of imagery in this poem similar or different to its use in another poem by Carol Ann Duffy you have read?	8
	To answer this you would choose one of the other set poems and comment on the use of imagery (simile, metaphor, personification). Think about what a 'typical' Carol Ann Duffy image looks like! In order to gain 7 or 8 marks you would need to construct a full answer supported by appropriate quotation/s.	
	Total	**20**

The Cone-Gatherers, by Robin Jenkins, pages 52–54

1.	How does the language of paragraph 1 (lines 1–23) help to suggest Lady Runcie-Campbell's state of mind at this point in the novel?	3
	You should mention at least two of the following. You would get 2 marks for each well-developed point you make (a reference to the language feature accompanied by a detailed comment on its effect) and 1 mark for a basic point. Your answer might include:	
	• List of verbs 'ran … stumbled, climbed … jumped … scrambled … plunged' in the first sentence suggests her feelings of urgency/ desperation.	
	• 'Surely just reasons for hating and despising them …' trying to convince herself.	
	• Long list separated by semi-colons of the reasons she gives herself.	
	• Repetition/triad/climax 'as a mother, as a landowner, as a Christian, even …' emphasises her attempts to justify her actions in her own mind.	
	• 'Yet' introduces a contrast – her inability to feel anger.	
	• List of emotions at the end of the paragraph 'Fear, anxiety, love, sorrow, regret, and hope' show how complex her feelings are.	

2.	Briefly describe the events that have led up to this point in the narrative.	2
	Lady Runcie-Campbell's son, Roderick in an attempt to emulate/show solidarity with the cone gatherers (1 mark) has climbed a tree and got stuck (1 mark).	
3.	How does the third paragraph (lines 28–35) help to illustrate an important theme of the novel?	2
	You should have noticed the references to the divisions between social classes that Jenkins criticises in the novel.	
	You could refer to any two of the following for 1 mark each:	
	• 'but it was a recognised rule of the world that if a subordinate was rewarded, his master must be rewarded also, to maintain stations, and of course more handsomely according to his higher degree' and how this reflects the society described in the novel.	
	• 'To maintain stations' echoes Lady Runcie-Campbell's husband's view of the world – a necessary hierarchy with the Runcie-Campbells at the top and the cone gatherers at the bottom.	
	• Jenkins clearly wants us to think this is wrong. The unfairness of artificial class distinctions is indicated by 'there were different medals for privates and officers, although they fought in the same battles'.	
4.	Why do you think Jenkins includes the reference to the warship in line 39?	2
	You should have spotted that this:	
	• echoes the reference to the warship in the description of setting at the beginning of the novel (1 mark)	
	• is also a reminder of the wider conflict taking place in the world beyond the estate (1 mark).	
5.	'... with so infinite a desolation in his every step' (line 56). How effective do you find this image used to describe Duror?	2
	Although you are always free to say something is not effective, it's generally easier to say that it is and support that view with appropriate comment and analysis. Here you could say that it's a very effective description and that the word 'infinite' suggests Duror's suffering seems endless (1 mark) and that 'desolation' suggests the feelings of emptiness and bleakness inside him that have not been removed by his killing of Calum (1 mark).	

6.	'She could not pray, but she could weep; and as she wept pity, and purified hope, and joy, welled up in her heart.' (lines 88–90) Why does Lady Runcie-Campbell react in this way? • Evil has been defeated through the sacrifice of Calum. • It is a moment of catharsis for her. • Her son is safe. • She thinks there is now hope for a better future. Any one of the above (1 mark).	1
7.	Calum is often described as a 'Christ-like' character. How does Jenkins suggest this to the reader? You should support your answer by referring to the extract and to the rest of the novel. You could mention a selection of the following points: • Calum's death 'twisted in the tree' echoes Christ's crucifixion. • Earlier in the novel Duror thinks that Calum must be removed and thinks of this as 'an agony' and 'a crucifixion'. • Calum's death (as Christ's was) is a necessary sacrifice to defeat evil and make the world a better place. • Calum's innocence, meekness and pity (including his empathy with other living creatures), referred to throughout the novel, are qualities he shares with Christ. • Calum is a symbol of goodness opposing the evil represented by Duror. You would get 1 mark for each basic point you made and 2 marks for a more developed point.	8
	Total	**20**

'Sounds of the Day', by Norman MacCaig, page 55

1.	Comment on the poet's use of sound in stanza 1 and stanza 2. You should refer to MacCaig's use of: • Onomatopoeia in 'clatter', 'creaked', 'snuffling puff', 'scraped' (1 mark). • Assonance, 'snuffling puff' (1 mark). • The finality of 'shut' ending in a sharp consonant (1 mark). • The words suggest a lively, (shared) imaginative engagement with the landscape (1 mark).	4

2.	How does MacCaig suggest the significance of the third stanza?	2
	Any two of:	
	• Its brevity, which adds impact (1 mark).	
	• The blunt/monosyllabic line 'You left me' (1 mark).	
	• The hyperbole of 'quietest fire in the world' to highlight the speaker's feelings of loss (1 mark).	
	• The contrast of quiet versus the sounds evoked in the first two stanzas (1 mark).	
3.	How does MacCaig use sentence structure to good effect in this poem?	4
	You could refer to:	
	• The repeated patterns in the first stanza 'When … It was … it was …' (1 mark) to highlight the variety of (imaginative) experiences and/or vivid description of the landscape (1 mark).	
	• The contrast between the shorter sentences in stanzas 2 and 3 and the longer sentence in the final stanza (1 mark).	
	• The longer sentence in the final stanza suggests the long-term effects of the emotional loss described in the poem (1 mark).	
4.	How effective do you find MacCaig's use of imagery in the final stanza?	2
	The imagery is striking and effective.	
	• The poet compares an emotional experience (losing someone) to a physical one (sticking your hand into icy water) (1 mark).	
	• 'bangle' suggests something decorative but also restrictive (1 mark).	
	• 'bangle' also suggests something circular/endless, perhaps referring to the speaker's feelings (1 mark).	
	• 'goes numb' suggests an absence of feeling, an emptiness, which echoes the absence of sounds after the loved one has gone (1 mark).	
	• Any two.	
5.	Show how the treatment of the theme of loss in this poem is similar or different to its treatment in another poem by MacCaig you have read.	8
	You could refer to poems such as 'Memorial' or 'Visiting Hour' in your answer. Your answer to this question would be 'marked on merit'. In order to get 7 or 8 marks for your answer you would need to provide a detailed response that made reference to specific features and poetic techniques (*word choice, tone, imagery, structure, content, rhythm, rhyme, theme, sound*) and offered a genuine comparison between 'Sounds of the Day' and your chosen poem.	